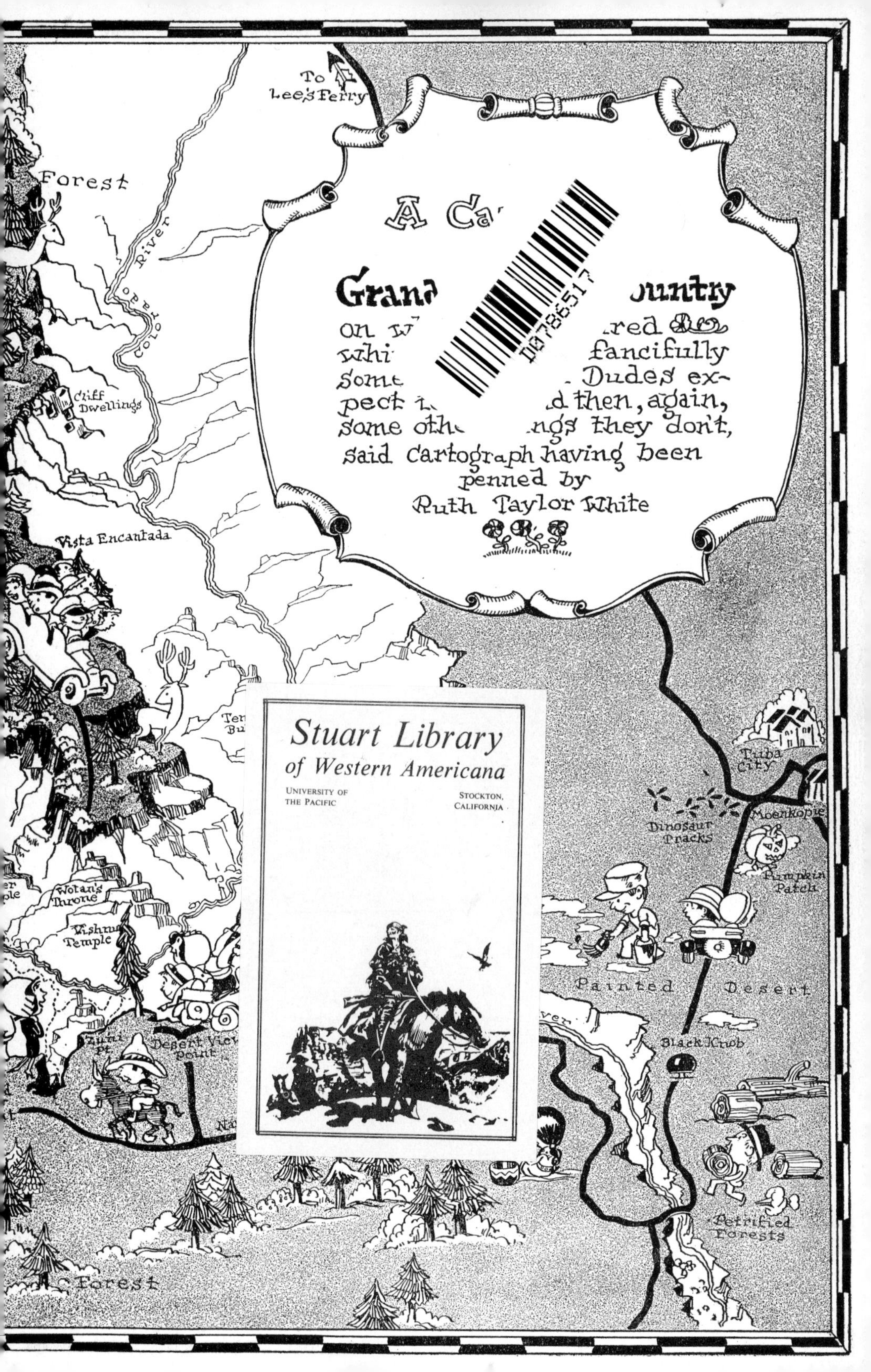
To Lee's Ferry
Forest
Colorado River
Cliff Dwellings
Vista Encantada
Wotan's Throne
Vishnu Temple
Zuni Pt.
Desert View Point
Tuba City
Moenkopie
Dinosaur Tracks
Pumpkin Patch
Painted Desert
Black Knob
Petrified Forests
Forest
A Ca
Grand ... ountry
on ... red
whi ... fancifully
some ... Dudes ex-
pect ... d then, again,
some othe ... ngs they don't,
said cartograph having been
penned by
Ruth Taylor White

GRAND CANYON COUNTRY

El Tovar Studio

"The Battleship," seen from El Tovar, South Rim

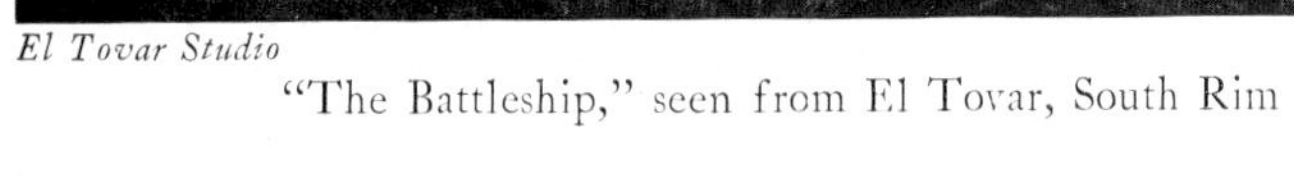

GRAND CANYON COUNTRY

BY

M. R. TILLOTSON

Superintendent Grand Canyon National Park

AND

FRANK J. TAYLOR

FOREWORD BY

HORACE M. ALBRIGHT

Director National Park Service
United States Department
of the Interior

1929

STANFORD UNIVERSITY PRESS
STANFORD UNIVERSITY, CALIFORNIA

Published 1929

PRINTED AND BOUND IN THE UNITED STATES
OF AMERICA BY STANFORD UNIVERSITY PRESS

FOREWORD

The Grand Canyon Country is one of the least known and appreciated of our national park areas, for the reason that people have had the habit of thinking of it merely as a colossal chasm. Simply viewing the Grand Canyon itself from one or the other of the rims of course has become a well-established habit among world travelers, as the result of publicity given to the colorful spectacle by agencies of travel and by the many writers who have attempted to put in words their emotions upon first seeing the Canyon.

I have always felt sorry for the traveler so rushed that he can see the Grand Canyon only from the rim. The descent into the great gorge is one of the real adventures of a lifetime. It is only by such a trip that one may know the Grand Canyon intimately or may appreciate the tremendous scope of this outstanding example of erosion.

Too many travelers to the Grand Canyon, moreover, have failed to take time to get acquainted with the fascinating country surrounding it—the Painted Desert, the land of the Navajos, and the pueblos of the Hopis, the ancient cliff dwellings, the petrified forests. It seems as if the Canyon itself had dwarfed these other wonders, any one of which, standing alone, would have been worth traveling to see.

I believe the authors of this book have shown rare judgment in not attempting to describe the Canyon adequately, for it cannot be done. Words are not equal to the task.

On the other hand, this book tells the story of the

Grand Canyon Country in a simple way and from an intimate point of view. It tells of the surrounding wonders that are often missed. I believe that anyone reading it will find himself revisiting the Canyon again and again, to explore anew on friendlier terms the by-ways of this fascinating region.

Of the authors, permit me to say simply that M. R. Tillotson, Superintendent of the Grand Canyon National Park, has done as much as any other individual to make the Grand Canyon Country a national playland, and he knows the Canyon area as does no other individual. And Frank J. Taylor has been closely associated with the National Parks for many years in such ways as to learn what the visitor wants to know. The imprint of the Stanford University Press is in itself sufficient indication of the reliability of this book.

HORACE M. ALBRIGHT
Director, National Park Service
United States Department of the Interior

WASHINGTON, D.C.
June 27, 1929

CONTENTS

LIST OF ILLUSTRATIONS

I. THE GRAND CANYON COUNTRY

One day a five-year old girl walked up to the rim of the Grand Canyon at El Tovar, gazed speechless at the sea of silent colors, then turned to her father with wonder in her eyes.

"Daddy," she asked, "what happened?"

That is precisely what every visitor to the Grand Canyon Country wants to know. It is a long story, one which has been millions of years in unfolding.

Long before the white man gazed with wonder at the Grand Canyon, generations of red men asked one another this same question, and their wise men evolved answers which were but the mythology of a primitive people.

The Navajo Indians, who have lived for many generations on the Painted Desert adjoining the Canyon to the east, told of a great flood, paralleling the biblical account. During this period of protracted rainfall, the Navajos say, the sea rose to great heights, and finally found an outlet for itself by cutting a gigantic chasm into the very depths of the earth. The Navajos say their ancestors were swept away by the rush of waters, but they did not perish, being turned temporarily into fish. With due respect to this adventure of their forebears, the older Navajos, to this day, refuse to eat fish.

Another Indian legend recounts the trials of a brave chieftain who had a young and beautiful bride, of whom he was extremely fond but who died only a short time after the marriage ceremony. The chieftain was beloved by the gods because of his reverence for them and because he ruled his people wisely and generously. His grief over the loss of his wife touched the hearts of the gods, and as a special concession they allowed him to visit her in the Spirit World, on condition that he would not reveal the route nor attempt the journey again. The trail followed along the bottom of the Grand Canyon, and to make sure that it would never be revealed, the gods turned into the Canyon the waters of the Great River, the Colorado.

Though these explanations of the Indian seem naïve and childish, they are as plausible in the light of modern scientific discovery as others advanced even today.

Not long ago an observing visitor, noting a jutting butte on the North Rim which appeared to be of the same size and shape as a certain amphitheater or side canyon on the South Rim, advanced the theory that "the Grand Canyon was formed by the north side being pulled away from the south side by some great force." What this force was and how it was applied, he did not say.

A persistent but mistaken idea ascribes the origin of the Canyon to contraction during the cooling of the earth's molten crust, at which time great cracks or fissures might be expected to develop in the molten mass. This theory might be accepted if any of the rock of the Canyon walls were a part of the earth's original crust. Instead, it is entirely sedimentary in origin.

There are those who believe that the presence of a great subterranean river, flowing through a vast cavern, the roof of which eventually fell in, led to the formation of the Canyon as it is today. A certain religious group hold that the Canyon was created by an earthquake which split the

El Tovar Studio

Grand Canyon from Grand Canyon Lodge, North Rim

Photo by A. R. Hromatka

Strata of the Canyon walls

Photo by A. R. Hromatka

Cloud shadows in the Canyon

earth open at the time of the crucifixion of Christ. Turning from the sublime to the ridiculous, there is the theory that a Scotchman lost a nickel in a gopher hole and is digging for it yet. This view is supported to a certain extent by the old lady who observed, after listening to a ranger naturalist's patient explanation of the millions of years of sedimentary deposit, followed by more millions of years of erosive action: "Well, young man, that sounds all right, but you can't make me believe this Canyon was dug without human help."

To satisfy the natural curiosity of visitors regarding the Grand Canyon, its formation, its geology, its history, its flora and fauna, the National Park Service maintains a museum near El Tovar and employs a staff of trained naturalists who are stationed near hotels and lodges on both the North and the South Rims.

These ranger-naturalists are frequently disputed by fundamentalists who accept their Bible literally and contend that the world is but six thousand years old and that it was made in six days, as per the account in the book of Genesis. They have accused the rangers of being sacrilegious infidels and occasionally prefer charges at the park headquarters.

The rangers have no choice but to accept the findings of geologists, and geologists are agreed about the Grand Canyon's origin. They regard it as the world's outstanding example of the work of the erosive forces of Nature, namely, the cutting action of running water, of frost, wind, and rain, abetted by chemical action, faulting, gravity, and growing vegetation.

One of the statements of the ranger-naturalists which

is often challenged is the remark that tiny rock plants have aided in carving the Canyon walls.

"But how can plants destroy rocks?" the visitor asks.

On the trails, one is impressed with the number of plants, notably lichens, to be seen growing on the bare rock surfaces. These primitive plants are, in a sense, small sponges, which catch rainwater and form weak carbonic acid, which starts disintegration of the limestone, until small holes are formed in the walls.

The tiny holes are then ready for the next plant succession, which are larger "sponges," retarding still more rain water, by which larger holes are dissolved. Eventually, there is formed in the hole, from the decay of moss or from dirt carried in by the winds or rains, enough soil to sustain a plant, which forces its roots down into the decomposing rock.

Water fills the holes thus formed. It naturally freezes and expands and next there appears a small crack, in which the seed of a piñon, a juniper, or a yellow pine may lodge and sprout. As the growing tree sways in the wind, its roots act as levers to pry the blocks of solid rock loose. Eventually they roll down the cliff, and the Canyon has been made that much wider.

This seems a terribly slow process. It is. But millions upon millions of plants have been digging away at the rocks for millions and millions of years. Time makes all things possible.

Temperature changes bring into play another slow but relentless action. The bare rock surfaces are warmed by the intensive rays of the desert sun, then chilled by the cool nights. This causes a continual expansion by day and contraction by night. Particles of rock flake off and crumble down the Canyon walls.

Another appreciable erosive agent is the wind, whipping around the cliffs during storms. The softer layers of sedimentary rock are particularly susceptible to wind erosion. In many places near the rims one may see where the winds have ground away the softer materials, leaving overhanging cliffs and windows in the rock. These overhanging cliffs were highly prized and much sought by primitive men, who walled up the outer edges and made for themselves cliff dwellings, remains of which may be found all along both rims of the Grand Canyon.

As the Grand Canyon country was lifted by some internal force of the earth, the pressure was unequal, resulting in great "faults" or cracks in the strata. A fault is a weakness along which the rocks disintegrate more rapidly, particularly if a stream of water flows through it.

Many of the great side canyons are the result of erosive action along faults. The most notable of these is the Bright Angel Fault, extending all the way from one rim to the other. Bright Angel Creek flows down this fault from the North Rim slope. Bright Angel Trail has been carved along the fault on the South Rim slope.

The bright colors of the Canyon walls are stains from the various minerals and mineral salts originally in the sediments. The reds are known as ferrous oxides. It is interesting to note that the thickest stratum of all, about half way down the Canyon walls, is known as "red-wall limestone." It was originally a steel blue-gray in color. Its present red color is a mere superficial stain from the iron oxides of the formation directly above.

The numerous "temples," so characteristic of Grand Canyon, are merely parts of the original plateau which, because of hard caps or the fickleness of the erosive agents, were able to withstand the destructive forces of Nature.

The Grand Canyon is the largest and most spectacular of a series of eighteen chasms through which the Colorado plunges its tortuous 1,600-mile trip from Wyoming to the Gulf of California. The Grand Canyon is 217 miles long.

The complete story of the formation of the Grand Canyon falls into two parts. The first is that of the building of the rock strata exposed to view today in the Canyon walls. The second tells of the wearing away of these rocks and the actual cutting of the gigantic chasm that is now the Grand Canyon.

The Grand Canyon itself is the world's most conspicuous example of erosion, or wearing away, by the combined forces of Nature. The formations of the Grand Canyon are the most interesting geological exhibits found in any limited area anywhere in the world. Each detail of form or color may be distinguished by the most casual observer.

The oldest rocks exposed are those at the bottom of the Canyon, namely, the crystalline schists, gneisses, and granitic rocks of the Archean Age. Since no older rocks are known in any part of the earth's surface, these are of special interest to the geologist. This formation was at one time subjected to great heat and internal pressure, and many portions of it are found in nearly vertical positions. Later the surface of these rocks was eroded to a plain by running water and weathering.

Next there came a submergence of this plain and the deposition in water of a series of sediments constituting the

Unkar and Chuar groups of the Algonkian period. These deposits slowly accumulated until they were some 12,000 feet in thickness. Then, following an extensive uplifting of the earth's crust, with tilting and faulting of the rocks, they became elevated above the surface of the ocean in which they were laid down. They were then still more slowly eroded away until at present only remnants of them may be seen.

When these two miles (vertical) or more of the Unkar and Chuar deposits had been reduced by erosion to a rolling plain with a few hills rising in places, there came another submergence in the sea, where was deposited the Tonto Group, the Tapeats Sandstone, the Bright Angel Shale, and the Muav Limestone of the Cambrian Age.

There then followed three important periods of geologic time, representing millions of years, of which the Canyon walls bear little or no record. The deposits laid down during the great Ordovician and Silurian periods are entirely missing, having been completely eroded away before the next sedimentation took place. The Devonian period, also, is represented only by small pockets of Temple Butte Limestone occasionally found at the top of the Muav Limestone.

In early Carboniferous time the entire region was again submerged by the sea, and there was deposited the calcium carbonate now represented by the 500 vertical feet of red-wall limestone of the Mississippian Age.

The deep submergence in which the red-wall limestone was laid down was followed in turn by comparatively shallow water, in which was deposited the Supai formation of the Pennsylvanian Age, containing some of the most primitive reptilian tracks, and likewise the Hermit Shale of the Permian Age.

Another decided change in geologic conditions was responsible for the formation of the 400-foot stratum of cross-bedded sandstone known as the Coconino. This is recognized as the best Permian fossil-track stratum in the world.

This last epoch was abruptly ended by another deep and long-continued submergence, during which there was laid down as a sedimentary deposit the calcium carbonate of the Permian Age, the present Kaibab Limestone. This is the topmost stratum of the Canyon walls and the level comprising the great plateau country—the surface of it as it is at present. Throughout this formation are found many species of marine fossils.

Sedimentation, however, did not cease with the formation of the Kaibab Limestone. It continued throughout the great Mesozoic Era, or "age of reptiles." It continued even into the Tertiary period, or the age when the primitive mammals were becoming dominant.

Geologists estimate that another deposit, from 6,000 to 7,000 feet in thickness, was originally laid down on top of the Kaibab Limestone, the present upper stratum of the Canyon walls.

Remains of this may be seen in Cedar Mountain, the flat-topped butte some two miles east of Desert View, and in Red Butte, which stands out alone from the surrounding comparatively flat country some eighteen miles south of El Tovar.

The complete succession of these younger formations is found in the Vermillion Cliffs, and in Zion and Bryce Canyon National Parks. Their removal by the slow process of erosion required several millions of years, and it was not until this removal was complete, or nearly so, that the actual work of cutting the Grand Canyon began.

Upon the removal by erosion of these younger formations, the Colorado River came into existence. If its present pattern may be taken as an indication, it was a sluggish meandering stream. Probably in the early history of the Canyon and at the time when the last great uplift began to take place, the river carried a greater volume of water than at present, especially during the time of the glacial retreat, when melting glaciers near the headwaters of the stream swelled the river and gave it a good start in cutting its way downward.

When mention is made of these uplifts and submergences, they should not be understood to be violent eruptions. They were gradual and slow changes in the elevation of the entire country, just as certain islands in the Pacific are today being raised and as portions of the Atlantic coast line are sinking.

The last great uplift of the region may still be in progress. It has raised the plateau to its present height, and this has occurred so gradually that the river has remained in its original channel.

As the elevation of the country has changed, the velocity of the river has increased proportionately, and since the silt-bearing power of water increases in proportion to its velocity, the river has carried more and more silt and has tumbled more rocks and boulders along the bottom of its channel.

Clear water has comparatively little cutting power. On the other hand, when water carries a vast amount of silt, sediment, loose gravel, and rolling rocks, these ingredients act as rasps in cutting the channel lower and lower. Throughout the length of the Canyon along the banks of the river may be seen huge boulders which have been carried down from above. At times of high water, these rocks set up a veritable roar, as they pound against each other and along the river bottom.

For eons the Colorado River has been carving away steadily at the Canyon walls. It is at present confined to the inner gorge, where it is still cutting its way downward; how fast, no one knows. So long as the fall of the stream bed and consequently the velocity of the water in the river is such that it can continue to carry away all of the sediment delivered to it by its tributaries, the river is certain to continue cutting its way downward, perhaps at the rate of a small fraction of an inch per year.

As the Grand Canyon now stands, it is a geologist's paradise, for nowhere else on the globe can he find, spread out before his eyes in well-marked layers, the story of the earth—at least, the story of the last few millions of years.

The Grand Canyon is a challenge to human curiosity, and legion are the questions asked of the park rangers each year by visitors. Here are some of them:

"How long did it take to do all this?"

That is a hard one to answer precisely! Geologists are fairly well agreed that it must have taken eight to ten million years for the river to cut the Canyon to its present size and depth. As one views the Grand Canyon he cannot help but be impressed by its magnitude. A full realization of the vast time interval during which the rocks composing the Canyon walls have been in process of formation, and of the millions of years it has taken for the Colorado River to cut its way downward to its present depth, is, however, vastly more impressive than the mere physical dimensions of the Canyon.

From rim to rim the Canyon averages eleven to thirteen miles, the narrowest width being four miles and the greatest eighteen. From some points on the Rim, the Colorado River may be seen, apparently a narrow ribbon; but those who make the trip down into the Canyon by trail are astonished to find it a swirling, roaring body of water from three hundred to four hundred feet wide.

The South Rim is nearly a mile above the river. The North Rim averages thirteen hundred feet higher. For the great plateau across which the Grand Canyon has been cut slopes from north to south.

Some queer notions exist regarding the size of the Canyon. One day the superintendent received a letter from a movietone company in New York City asking if he would pose for a picture on the South Rim and be telling a party of Dudes about the Grand Canyon. The letter concluded:

"At the end we want the visitors on the South Rim and another group on the North Rim to talk back and forth exclaiming over the wonders of the Canyon."

Bantering across ten miles of space would call for some higher-powered bantering than anyone has been able to do yet. As a matter of fact, the great chasm seems to swallow all sound, and more than one visitor has gazed, enraptured by the silence, on the rim and then exclaimed: "Why, it's so silent you can hear it!"

"Will Boulder Dam fill the Grand Canyon with water?"

Every visitor wants this point settled in his mind. The dam site is 198 miles below the western boundary of the park, via the river course. Even when the dam reaches a height of 550 feet, as proposed, the waters of the river will be backed up to a point 80 miles from the park. Consequently, the construction of Boulder Dam will not affect the Grand Canyon in any way.

The weather down in the Canyon is one of the surprises of the Grand Canyon. It may be snowing on the rims, while at Phantom Ranch and at the foot of the Kaibab Trail, a mile below, visitors will be enjoying semitropical temperature. One mile in altitude is the equivalent of about eight hundred miles of latitude—consequently, the bottom of the Canyon enjoys a climate similar to that of Imperial Valley, while the rims have that of the Rocky Mountain area. Valleys in side chasms off the Grand Canyon are semitropical the year around.

The area surrounding the Grand Canyon is almost as interesting, if not as spectacular, as the great chasm itself. It is one of Nature's greatest storehouses of geologic phenomena. Here is spread out a picture-story of the earth, a moving picture to the visiting motorist.

East from the South Rim lies "El Desierto Pintado," the Painted Desert, as the early Spanish explorers so aptly named it. A magnificent stretch of strange earth formations, in many shades, that change with the receding sunlight, it is one of the earth's most fascinating spots. Its fantastically shaped rocks, flat buttes, weather-worn pillars, enchanted mesas, pastel shades of every color, softly and smoothly blended, cause one to wonder if he has not suddenly slipped into some dreamland.

II. DISCOVERY AND EXPLORATION

The Grand Canyon was the first of the great American natural wonders now preserved as national parks to be discovered by white men. It was in 1540, only forty-eight years after Columbus discovered America, that one Don Lopez de Cardenas, with twelve hardy conquistadores, stood on the brink of the South Rim and gazed speechless across the Grand Canyon.

Don Lopez was disappointed! He had struggled across hot deserts looking for the fabled "seven cities of gold" and had found only an impenetrable chasm. Certain of his soldiers attempted to descend into the Canyon to the river but failed. Turning their faces toward Mexico, the Spaniards remembered seeing rocks which from the rim "appeared about as tall as a man," but which were found by those who attempted to descend to the river to be "taller than the great tower of Seville."

That is probably the first recorded impression of the Grand Canyon. The disappointment of the discoverers is indicated by the fact that 236 years, seven or eight generations, elapsed before the Canyon was again visited by the Spanish. It lay unmolested, the almost legendary northwestern boundary of Tusayan Province, as the Spanish called what is now Arizona and New Mexico.

To recapitulate a bit of history, Spain, after Columbus' momentous discovery, was aflame with the spirit of conquest. Cortez conquered Mexico. Pizarro seized Peru. Both brought back gold and silver. Pinedo explored the shores of the Gulf of Mexico, from Florida to Mexico, returning with tales of rich cities to the north.

Narvaez, eager for wealth, seeking these fabled cities, marched overland from the Gulf. He and all but four of his men perished. The four, Alvar Nuñez Cabeza de Vaca in charge, after amazing adventures including frequent capture by Indians, made the perilous trip afoot from the Mississippi to Mexico, reaching Culican, Spanish frontier outpost, in 1536 after six years of wandering.

De Vaca's tales of his 2,000-mile overland trip, and of the land rich in gold described to him by the Indians, led the Viceroy of Mexico, Antonio de Mendoza, to send the Franciscan monk Fray Marcos de Nizza with a handful of soldiers on an exploring expedition into what is now New Mexico. Fray Marcos started in 1539.

There was an old Spanish legend, generally believed at this time, that in the eighth century, when the Moslems conquered the Spanish Peninsula, a certain bishop of Lisbon with his followers took refuge in a land far to the west, beyond the Sea of Darkness, where they founded cities of vast wealth, the fabled Seven Cities of Cibola.

Early in his trip, Fray Marcos was told by the Indians that "seven large cities, with houses of stone" would be found thirty days march to the north. Quite naturally, the eager padre assumed these were the much-sought "cities of Cibola." He pushed on to a group of seven Zuñi pueblos, forty miles south of the present site of Gallup, New Mexico, confident that the dreams of Spain were about to be realized.

One of the companions of Fray Marcos was Estevanico, "Little Stephen," a negro, who had accompanied de Vaca

Photo by Willard S. Wood

The Painted Desert, seen from the Navahopi Road

Union Pacific Photo

The Canyon and river from Toroweap Point, North Rim

Fred Harvey Photo

The Canyon from the new Desert View Road

in his wanderings. Ambitious to be the first to discover the Seven Cities, Estevanico had pushed on ahead of the party. Thus it was that the first "white man" to enter what is now Arizona was a negro. Just before Fray Marcos reached Zuñi, however, he was met by Estevanico's Indian guide, in precipitous flight. The Indian declared that Estevanico had actually reached Cibola but that the natives had put him to death. Alarmed, the padre returned to Mexico and reported he had located the famed Seven Cities but could not enter them.

Great was the excitement in Mexico. The gallant officer, Francisco de Coronado was placed at the head of three hundred Spanish soldiers and eight hundred Mexican Indians, to conquer the Seven Cities. Marching north to Zuñi, he was chagrined to discover but a group of poor Indian villages.

From them, however, he learned of the great country of Tusayan, present home of the Hopi Indians, lying to the northwest. Coronado dispatched Don Pedro de Tovar and a group of twenty men to explore. Arriving at Walapai and Oraibi, they discovered thriving Hopi villages, but no gold.

Returning to their command, they so reported and repeated the Hopi tale of "the great river" lying still farther to the west. To verify this story, Coronado dispatched Cardenas with the twelve men who first gazed into the colorful Grand Canyon in 1540.

Small wonder then that the Spaniards, after these futile efforts, abandoned interest in the Grand Canyon country!

History makes no further mention of the region for 236 years, until 1776, when it was visited by two Spanish priests, Padre Garces and Padre Escalante. On their trip eastward from the Lower Colorado they visited the Havasupai Indians who lived then as now in the depths of the beautiful and picturesque Havasu Canyon.

They halted "at the sight of the most profound caxones which ever onward continue, and within these flows the Colorado." On this trip they crossed the Colorado River at the old Ute Ford, near the head of Glen Canyon and known thereafter as *El Vado de los Padres*—the Crossing of the Fathers.

Quest of beaver pelts brought to the Grand Canyon the first Americans of record, James O. Pattie and his father, who in 1825 trapped up the Colorado River and its tributaries from its junction with the Gila. Suffering from lack of food, and after battles with Indians, the Patties made their way east along the rim of the Canyon. Theirs is the first recorded trip along either rim of the Canyon.

There are reports of visits to the region by General Ashley and by the famous American trapper and explorer, Jedediah Smith, who blazed a trail to California in 1826. Kolb (see below, page 25) reports that the name "D. Julian, Mai, 1836" is carved on the walls in Labyrinth Canyon and again in Cataract Canyon. However, the first authentic report on the Grand Canyon and its magnitude was made by Lieutenant J. C. Ives, who in 1858 was detailed by the War Department to explore the "Colorado River of the West" and ascertain how far up it was navigable.

Reaching the head of navigation at the foot of Black Canyon, a detail returned to Yuma with the small stern-wheel iron steamer, "Explorer," while Ives and a few of his companions went through the Black Canyon in a rowboat to the mouth of Las Vegas Wash.

He then descended the river until he met a pack train which had followed him as far as possible up the bank of the stream. Here he disembarked and on March 24, 1858, started with a land party guided by the Mojave chief, Iritaba, to explore the eastern bank of the river. Making a long detour, he ascended to the top of the plateau, obtained views of the Canyon along its lower course, and visited, on April 14, the home of the Havasupai Indians, now within Grand Canyon National Park.

The geologist with the Ives expedition was Dr. J. S. Newbury. His was the first geological explanation and description of the Canyon and the plateau through which it is cut. His report stimulated wide interest in the Canyon.

The famous Mormon pioneer, scout, and trail blazer, Jacob Hamblin, the "Leatherstocking of the Southwest," had the surprising experience of seeing the little steamer "Explorer" on the Colorado River in the course of one of his numerous missions into the Grand Canyon country.

In the fall of 1858, Hamblin headed an expedition to the Hopi Indian country to investigate, at the order of Brigham Young, President of the Mormon State, a rumor to the effect that the Hopi dialect embraced many Welsh words. The Mormon leader had received reports that, centuries before, a group of Welshmen had disappeared into the Western wilds and that it was thought that this party was either responsible for the origin of the Hopi tribe or that they had been absorbed by the Hopis, thus accounting for the presence of Welsh words in the Indian tongue.

One member of Hamblin's party, Ammon M. Tenney, was a Welshman familiar with the language of his native land, and although only fifteen years old he spoke a number of Indian dialects, as well as Spanish. A diligent investigation was made by the two, Hamblin and Tenney, but no Hopi word was found that was similar in any wise to Welsh or any other European language.

As a matter of fact, the Hopi tongue is a composite, mainly a Shoshonean dialect. The Hamblin party of 1858 crossed the Colorado River near the mouth of Paria Creek, later the site of Lee's Ferry. En route to the Hopi villages they lost the pack mules carrying the provisions. The hungry Mormons were received with hospitality by the Hopis, who furnished them with food until their runaway mules were brought in.

At the direction of Brigham Young, Hamblin again visited the Hopi country in 1859 and once more in 1862, when he crossed the Colorado south of St. George in the hope of finding a passable route to the south. It was the Mormon ambition to found a great state in the arid southwest, by means of outpost colonies, which could develop irrigation projects. Settlements north of the Grand Canyon, in what was known as "Utah's Dixie" because of its tropical climate and products, were successful; but the Mormons never found their hoped-for easy route to southern Arizona.

Hamblin records that at the Indian villages the Hopis "had been going through some religious ceremonies to induce the Great Spirit to send storms to water their country, that they might raise an abundance of food for the coming season." This is the earliest recorded reference to the annual Hopi Snake Dance.

In March 1863 Hamblin again started from St. George with a party of six men and this time located a new and better crossing of the Colorado called Pearce's Ferry. On this trip Hamblin traversed the Walapai country and into Havasu Canyon, where he noted the beautiful waterfalls and the irrigated lands of this friendly tribe. The party left Havasu Canyon by way of the Topocoba Trail, which is still in use.

The fastnesses of the Canyon served frequently in early days as the hiding places of fugitives from justice. On the North Rim one side canyon, still known as Robber's Roost, was occupied for years by a band of highwaymen and cattle rustlers. The old Tanner trail from the base of Lipan Point on the South Rim was in the early days known as the "Horsethief Trail."

One small side canyon on the South Rim just west of Rowe's Well is shown on the maps as "Horsethief Canyon." An old cattleman, now a resident of Flagstaff, stated that the name of this canyon was a direct and personal insult to him, because he was the first and only man ever to occupy this canyon and he "could lick the man that ever called him a hoss thief."

One of the most notorious characters ever to be identified with the Grand Canyon was John D. Lee, leader of the famous Mountain Meadows Massacre, in which on September 11, 1857, an emigrant train from Arkansas en route to the Pacific Coast was entirely wiped out by a band of Indians. History concedes now that Lee was merely a renegade and that the massacre was conceived and executed entirely by him. Lee became a fugitive from justice and finally, in 1872, located on the Colorado River at the mouth of Paria Creek. There he built a log cabin and acquired ferry rights that had been possessed formerly by the Mormon Church. Today "Lee's Ferry" is a historic landmark. Prior to this Lee had spent two or three years hiding among the Havasupai Indians. He is credited with having planted the fruit seeds from which sprang the Indian orchards there.

United States troops continued their search for Lee for years. He was captured eventually while on a trip for provisions to the settlements of southern Utah. Tried and convicted, he was executed by a firing squad in March 23, 1877; ironically enough, when shot he was seated on his coffin at the very spot where he led the massacre.

The first systematic exploration of the Grand Canyon was made by Major John Wesley Powell, the one-armed hero of the Civil War Battle of Shiloh and later director of the United States Geological Survey. Powell's account of his trip through the unknown Canyon is an epic of American achievement and literature.

Determined efforts were made by friends, pioneers, and even the Indians to dissuade Powell from his hazardous voyage. Friends asserted he was attempting an impossible venture. Pioneers warned of the helplessness of the tiny boats in the angry, ruthless rapids and whirlpools. Indians foretold the anger of the Great Spirit and cited legends to prove that the river flowed for many miles into forbidding underground passages.

Undaunted, Powell left Green River, Wyoming, hundreds of miles above the Grand Canyon, on May 24, 1869, with nine men and four boats. The nine courageous companions were W. H. Powell, the Major's younger brother, J. C. Somner, William H. Dunn, G. Y. Yardley, O. G. Howland, Seneca Howland, his brother, Frank Goodman, W. R. Hawkins, and Andrew Hall.

The hardships endured by Powell and his men, their helplessness in the tiny boats, rushing through mad rapids and whirlpools in deep canyons, their weary portages around waterfalls, the lonesomeness of their isolation, the never-ending roar of the hungry waters, the days on end spent in damp clothing, the meagerness and monotony of their fare, and the mental hazard of their courageous trip are all set forth with rare simplicity by the self-effacing Powell in his book, *First through the Grand Canyon.*

At every turn Powell made calculations with such instruments as were not lost or hopelessly damaged in the numerous upsets in the rapids. In spite of the handicap of the loss of one arm, he scaled the sheer lower walls of the Canyon almost daily to study the terrain above. It is to Powell that we are indebted for many of the amazingly appropriate and descriptive names of Grand Canyon temples and canyons and creeks.

Three months from the day the voyage started, his greatest catastrophe overtook Powell. Three men, the Howland brothers and William H. Dunn, deserted the expedition. Convinced that it was folly to attempt to go farther, they left the party and chose to scale the cliffs and brave the desert rather than go on like flotsam down the muddy, raging river. When the party divided, in good spirit, each group thought the other was headed for death. One group was—the three who deserted were killed by Indians, who mistook them for marauding miners.

The strength of his party weakened, Powell abandoned one of his boats and pushed on in three bobbing skiffs. It was the irony of fate that at noon of the very next day after the desertion, Powell and his men, with a shout of unrestrained joy, rounded a bend and beheld before them the smooth waters of the Lower Colorado. They were out of the Canyon! Shortly thereafter they reached the Virgin River and its Mormon settlements, where they secured much-needed sustenance and clothing.

Undaunted by his harrowing adventure and lured by the spell of the Canyon, Major Powell made an overland trip in the spring of 1870 and spent the summer in exploring ways down to the river from the North Rim. The following spring he again started down stream with three boats, descending as far as the Crossing of the Fathers, where he left the river, and, with a pack train, spent the summer, fall, winter, and following spring exploring the country north of the river. In 1872 he returned once more to the point where he had cached his boats the previous spring and descended through Marble Canyon and the Grand Canyon as far as the mouth of Kanab Wash, there abandoning the river journey.

In subsequent years, he continued the exploration of the country adjacent to the Grand Canyon. On these trips Napoleon Gilbert, Captain C. E. Dutton, and Professor A. H. Thompson, noted geologists, accompanied him. In 1882, Major Powell and C. D. Walcott, the latter likewise later the Director of the United States Geological Survey, entered the Canyon by means of a trail which they constructed down Nankoweap Creek. Walcott and a small party of men were left in the Canyon for the entire winter making a complete and systematic geological survey of the region.

In later years, other daring adventurers attempted the trip, some successfully, some shadowed by death.

Frank M. Brown and Robert B. Stanton left Greenriver, Utah, on May 25, 1889, with sixteen men and six very light boats. The purpose of this trip was to make a survey for a railroad which it was proposed to build from western Colorado to tidewater. The trip was temporarily abandoned in lower Marble Canyon, and was re-outfitted, December 28, 1889. Disaster hovered over this expedition. Frank M. Brown, the leader, and two other men were drowned in Marble Canyon. F. A. Nims sustained a broken leg in a fall and it was necessary to carry him out over a seventeen-hundred-foot wall to a point on the plateau which could be reached by wagon. The rest of the party, under Stanton, finally reached the Gulf of California on April 26, 1890.

Nathan Galloway left Green River, Wyoming, in the fall of 1895 and descended as far as Lee's Ferry. Again in 1896 he and William Richmond left Henry's Fork, Wyoming, and reached Needles, California, February 10, 1897.

On August 27, 1896, George F. Flavell and one companion left Green River, Wyoming, on a trapping and prospecting expedition, reaching Yuma, Arizona, with one flat-bottom boat in December 1897.

Charles S. Russell, E. R. Monette, and Bert Loper left Greenriver, Utah, September 20, 1907. Loper's boat was punctured in Cataract Canyon, where he remained to make necessary repairs while the others continued on their prospecting trip, as far as Lee's Ferry. After a long wait there they proceeded without Loper, who arrived some time later but discontinued the trip when he found that his companions had gone on. A second boat was lost in the Hance Rapids and the third was torn loose while it was being lined through the Hermit Creek Rapids. Russell and Monette climbed the Granite Gorge and arrived finally at the camp of Louis Bouchre, a prospector. One of their boats was found the following day with three holes in its side in a whirlpool five miles below Hermit Creek Rapids. After making repairs, they continued their trip to Needles, which they reached in February 1908.

On September 12, 1909, Julius F. Stone of Columbus, Ohio, left Greenriver, Utah, with a party of three men, including Nathan Galloway as chief boatman. The purpose of this trip was photographic exploration, and the remarkable record was made of having brought two boats through without a single upset. The party arrived at Needles on November 19, 1909, with no fatalities and with both boats in good condition. Galloway, mention of whose previous trip has already been made, had descended the river through the Uinta Valley five times, through Desolation and Gray Canyons seven times, through Cataract Canyon three times, and through the Grand Canyon once before making this trip with Stone.

On September 8, 1911, Emery C. Kolb, with his brother, Ellsworth L., and James Fagin, outfitted at Greenriver, Utah, with two flat-bottom boats, the "Defiance" and the "Edith," and arrived at the foot of Bright Angel Trail November 16, 1911, Fagin having left the party at the foot of Lodore Canyon. On December 19, the trip to Needles was continued, Hubert R. Lauzon, now a park ranger in Grand Canyon National Park, joining the party for the rest of the trip. Lauzon finished the trip at Needles with the Kolb brothers on January 18, 1912. E. L. Kolb, in May 1913, continued the trip from Needles to the Gulf, traveling on the high water and making the four-hundred-mile run in eight days. The purpose of this trip was the taking of Canyon photographs, and on this river voyage were made the first motion pictures of the Grand Canyon and its rapids. These motion pictures may be seen at Kolb Studio, near El Tovar, on the South Rim.

There are also shown motion pictures taken during a Government trip made in 1923 by the United States Geological Survey for the purpose of making a survey of possible dam sites. Emery C. Kolb was chief boatman on this Government trip.

In 1927 a successful trip was made down the river from Greenriver, Utah, to Hermit Creek by the Eddy Party for the purpose of taking motion pictures. Many additional attempts to traverse the rapids of the Colorado River have ended in death and disaster, including that of Glen R. Hyde and his wife, who lost their lives while on a honeymoon trip down the river in December 1928.

The National Park Service discourages this as a pleasure trip, and urgently recommends that it be attempted by none except those making it in the interest of science, accompanied by experienced river men, and provided with the best possible equipment.

In spite of the fact that the earliest exploration of the Canyon dates back to 1540 and that in the meantime it has been visited by many exploring parties and hundreds of thousands of tourists, there are still many side canyons and isolated buttes where "the hand of man has never set foot," as the Old-Timer remarked.

The National Park Service is engaged continuously in an exploration of these unknown regions, for the purposes of securing geological and other specimens, of searching for and recording cliff dwellings and other evidences of prehistoric human existence, and of securing data on the flora and fauna of the region. It was while they were engaged on an exploration of this kind that Glen E. Sturdevant, park naturalist, and Fred Johnson, ranger, lost their lives in line of duty on February 20, 1929.

III. INDIANS AND THEIR CUSTOMS

Indians of the Grand Canyon country are one of its most fascinating lures. The district is one of the very few areas in the United States where the red man still lives in his native state, primitive but happy, contented, unchanged by the white man's civilization.

In addition, the Grand Canyon region bears many mute evidences of a prehistoric people who lived in strange cliff dwellings high in the prismatic walls of the side canyons. Who these people were, whence they came, and what happened to them remains a mystery, despite the earnest investigations and studies of scholars.

That these prehistoric peoples who beat trails into the Canyon long before white men ever gazed upon it attained a fair standard of living is evidenced by the relics they have left in their dwellings—mealing stones, earthen vessels, ornaments, bits of pottery, and articles of wearing apparel, notably homespun cotton cloth and sandals made from the fiber of the yucca plant.

Almost invariably, these cliff dwellings were constructed by piling stones, secured by a mud mortar, along the outer edges of shelves protected by large overhanging rocks. Most of them were reached only by narrow trails along precarious ledges, indicating that the occupants sought safety there from marauding enemies.

The cliff dwellers evidently cultivated small plots of soil on the flats below and carried their crops in baskets on their shoulders to their isolated fortress homes.

Cliff dwellings of the Grand Canyon were probably family affairs, thus differing from those of the Mesa Verde National Park, which were generally large enough to accommodate a good-sized village. Some to be seen along the Canyon are but tiny quarters, sufficient to shelter three or four Indians, a mere niche in the side of the cliff.

These ruins may be found in almost any part of the park. A ten-minute walk from Grand Canyon Lodge on the North Rim brings one to an old cliff dwelling in excellent state of preservation. Several may be seen from the road between El Tovar on the South Rim and Desert View.

On the wall of Cape Royal is one of the finest cliff-dwelling sites, a broad ledge, overhung by an enormous boulder, at the foot of which flows a crystal spring. Unfortunately, the works left here by pre-historic peoples were molested in early days by the cattle rustlers who used the trail past this dwelling.

On Nankoweap Creek, in the northeastern corner of the park, are a number of large and well-preserved cliff dwellings. Several, together with mescal pits and food caches, may be seen from the Kaibab Trail in Bright Angel Canyon and others are found near Ribbon Falls, Shinumo Creek, and Clear Creek—human habitations long before America was dreamed of!

An idea of these strange homes may be gleaned from reports made by park rangers who have examined the remains of dwellings and "kivas," ceremonial chambers, at Clear Creek. The largest rooms were sixteen by forty feet in size. Their slowly crumbling walls still stood four feet high. One of the larger chambers was reached by a flight of stone steps showing real architectural skill.

That this dwelling had been occupied for many decades, perhaps centuries, was indicated by relics of pottery of four distinct types. A mealing stone, worn almost in two, and a "mano," or grinding stone, reduced to a mere shell, bore mute evidence of the generations of industrious hands which on this spot had ground tons of corn to meal.

The discovery of corncobs and dried pods resembling a giant lima bean in ancient food caches gives an inkling of the agricultural pursuits of these lost peoples. The caretaker of Kaibab Trail found some of these beans in a dwelling on Bright Angel Creek; planted by a cabin near Phantom Ranch, they germinated and produced lusty vines which covered the entire front of the cabin.

The patience with which the cliff dwellers labored may be realized after inspection of frequent small flat areas along the lower Bright Angel Trail, formed and fenced with low rock walls. These were the tiny garden patches of people who sought safety and shelter in dwellings high above on the cliffs. Numerous mescal pits, circles of fire-blackened stones, reveal that the cliff dwellers were fond of the roasted mescal, the succulent pineapple-shaped bud of *Agave utahensis*. The Kaibab Trail passes by many of these blackened pits, and directly through one ten feet in diameter. It is located one mile above Ribbon Falls, on the North Rim slope.

These cliff dwellers may have been the forerunners of the present-day Indians who thrive in the Grand Canyon country, or they may have been a lost race, who perished from the earth notwithstanding their ingenuity in sheltering and protecting themselves.

The pottery and other relics left by the cliff dwellers

bear resemblance to the present-day works of the Hopis. The mescal pits are used today only by the Havasupais. Both of these tribes are tillers of the soil, as were the ancient cliff dwellers.

All Indians who inhabit the region adjacent to the Grand Canyon belong to one of three tribes, Navajo, Hopi, or Havasupai. The Navajos are the Bedouins of the southwest, continually roaming the desert with their flocks of sheep and goats. The Hopis live in pueblos, or towns, on the mesas overlooking the fields which they irrigate and cultivate. The Havasupais are the River Indians, living far down on the flats in the narrow canyons bordering on the Colorado.

Strictly speaking, the Havasupais are the only Indians who make their homes in the park proper, though the others come to the Canyon to work and to sell their wares.

The Havasupai Reservation is in Havasu or Cataract Canyon, a tributary of the Grand Canyon, near the western end of the park. It may be reached only by a fourteen-mile trail trip from the rim. These Indians are related to the Yumas, farther to the west. Their name, meaning "people of the blue water," is derived from the brilliant color of the lime-impregnated water of Havasu Creek.

In an earlier period of its existence, the tribe lived along the Little Colorado River, and later in the San Francisco Mountains. A peaceful people, they were no match for the warlike Apaches who surrounded them, and the Havasupais fled finally to the canyons of the Colorado for safety.

At one time they cultivated numerous flats of land along the river. A small band lived at what is now called Indian Gardens, on Bright Angel Trail below El Tovar.

Fred Harvey Photo

The Hight Wall

Fred Harvey Photo

A Navajo silversmith at work before his hogan

Camera Study by Mode Wineman

Havasupai Indian huts in Havasu Canyon

In more recent years they have concentrated at Havasu Canyon, where Padre Garces reported them flourishing in 1776.

The total strength of the tribe is but 185, near which figure it has remained stationary for many years. The home of the Havasupais is a beautiful, level canyon floor, about two and one-half miles long and one-half mile wide, through which flows Cataract Creek. The creek rises a few miles above the Indian village in a series of springs, and plunges through Havasu Canyon in a series of three waterfalls, one of them two hundred feet in height.

In this haven of refuge, the fertile soil, an abundance of water, and a semi-tropical climate enable the Havasupais to raise all they need of grain, alfalfa, corn, melons, fruits, and vegetables.

Of all native tribes in the United States, this remnant of a timid, peace-loving people is least touched by civilization from the outside. The older men of the tribe tell how time after time, in the olden days, the Apaches raided the canyon, drove out the Havasupais, and stole their stores of food. Time after time, the river people returned to their valley and industriously planted new crops. It is the proud boast of the Havasupais that no member of their tribe ever killed a white man.

The Havasupais are good farmers but are not as skilled as their neighbors, the Navajos or the Hopis, though the women make fair baskets, some of which are covered with piñon pitch to serve as water jars.

The men are honest, industrious workers, much in demand by the National Park Service for trail and road construction. They need no boss to keep them working at simple labor, though they refuse to burden themselves with thinking.

One day a foreman in charge of the digging of a trench instructed a group of Havasupais to dig according to grade, which point he indicated very carefully. Returning, the foreman found the Indians had ignored grade, but had kept on digging.

"Don't you savvy grade?" the foreman asked.

"No savvy," the lead Indian said.

"Well, what do you savvy?" the foreman demanded.

"Just diggin'," the Indian replied.

The Havasupais cannot be bothered with the advantages of civilization. They have resisted every effort of the Indian agents to provide better homes, preferring their rude huts. At one time, the Government undertook to build each Havasupai family a cottage. The Indians, using these for storehouses and for their farm implements, continued to live in their old huts.

One of the most interesting sidelights on the Havasupais, aside from their unaffected primitive life and picturesque surroundings, is their ceremony of roasting the mescal. This is done after the manner of the prehistoric cliff dwellers, except that the Havasupais use a rectangular instead of a circular mescal pit.

Among the Havasupais, the plant is known as "veyel." It is gathered in the spring after the bud has started. When a considerable supply has been collected, a mescal pit three feet long, two feet wide, and three and a half feet deep is prepared, then filled with water-worn rocks, on top of which the firewood is piled. The fire must be lighted, according to tribal customs, by some member whose birthday occurs in the summer, or the "veyel" would never cook but would remain white and tasteless rather than turn the desired brown with the sickly sweetish taste so pleasing to the Havasupai palate.

After the fire has burned until the rocks are heated and blackened with ashes, the rocks are tamped by dropping a huge boulder repeatedly into the pit, the veyel plants are piled on, and over them is laid a layer of grass and then one of earth. During the roasting, the Indians paint their faces with a red pigment, to assure a good roasting. This paint may not be removed until an older member of the tribe, designated official tester, pronounces the food properly cooked.

The bottom part of the veyel when chewed yields a sweet syrup. The upper part is served as a sweet bread, while the asparagus-like leaves are ground and baked with corn as a cake. Preparing this food will probably become a lost art in another generation, for the reason that younger Havasupais are developing the taste for the white man's delicacies, so much more easily provided by opening a can or a jar.

The Navajos are the most virile and the most prosperous of all the Southwestern Indians. They have been steadily increasing in numbers until today there are about 40,000 of them on the Navajo Reservation of 9,500,000 acres. However, because of their nomadic habits, Navajos are never seen together in great numbers.

"Apaches de Navajoa" was the name applied to the tribe by the early Spanish explorers, probably because of their resemblance to the warlike Apaches. Navajoa is the name of what was then a frontier town in Sonora, Mexico.

Except in talking to whites, the Navajos never refer to themselves by that name. Among themselves they are "Dene," or "Tinneh," meaning "the people," and they believe themselves to be far superior to all other Indian tribes.

Originally warlike and predatory, the Navajos for centuries captured and assimilated into their tribe women and children of the Hopis, the Zuñis, the Shoshones, and the River Indians. As the result of this practice, there is no distinct Navajo type. Some have the broad faces of the Apaches, some the high noses and general features of the Plains Indians, and others almost Asiatic characteristics. The Navajo speaks a distinct tongue and talks of a traditional home to the north. Exactly when or whence he came, he has no knowledge.

Among those who know him, the Navajo is admired for his lofty independence. He can, if occasion demands, look straight through a white man without seeing him, as if the latter were too inferior to be noticed by one of "the people." He carries himself with dignity, but underneath this he is good-humored, even gay.

The Navajo lives out under the skies the year around. A nomad, he is ever on the move, with his family and his flocks. He spends much of his time on horseback. His home is his campfire. Sometimes, if time permits and the weather is bad, he builds a rude log and mud hut, or hogan, resembling a beehive open at the top, about his flickering flames, or makes use of a predecessor's hogan. The deserts about the Canyon are dotted with these crude circular dwellings, doors always facing east. Following his flock from one pasture to another, the Navajo camps in a hogan, if he can find one; if not, he builds his campfire in the shelter of a ravine or a cliff.

If plentiful grass leads him to pause at any time in his wanderings, the Navajo generally builds for himself a new brush hogan if it is summer or one of logs if it is winter. For plaster to keep out the night winds, he uses mud. If death overtakes any member of his tribe in a hogan, it is "tsindi" and must be abandoned or burned. For this reason, whenever possible the mortally ill are carried outside the hut to die!

Navajo legends tell of the introduction of sheep and goats into the life of the tribe by capture from the early Spanish settlers in Mexico, probably in the sixteenth century. Before that, the tribe lived no doubt by hunting and by raiding their more industrious neighbors. Today there is scarcely a family that does not possess several hundred sheep, and many Navajos own thousands.

Sheep and goats are watched over by the women and children. By custom, they are all the property of the wife. Navajo women watch over the sheep tenderly. In cold weather, the little lambs are taken into the hogans and wrapped in blankets, and it is not unusual for a Navajo woman to nurse from her own breast a motherless lamb.

Horses, saddles, and other equipment, even though used by the women, are the property of the men; likewise all jewelry, which is generally made by the men, the Navajos being skilled silversmiths.

A Navajo woman may divorce her husband by the simple expedient of placing his saddle outside the hogan door, but this almost never happens. Navajo family ties are strong and Navajos are devoted to their children.

Originally a Navajo had the right to as many wives as he could purchase and support, but polygamy is disappearing under the white man's law. Wives are obtained by purchase, negotiations being made between the prospective groom and his equally prospective mother-in-law, the girl in the case having no word in the matter.

Recently the superintendent of the Navajo Reservation found an old Navajo in a remote corner of the reservation with several wives. Very carefully the superintendent explained that this was contrary to law and told the old Indian to return to his home, look over his wives, pick out the one he wanted to keep, and then tell the others they were no longer his spouses.

The old Navajo listened quietly and patiently to this explanation, then spoke for the first time, saying: "Huh! You tell 'em!"

The Navajos have no head chief. The tribe is composed of some ten or twelve clans, each of which has its leader, or head-man, chosen for his superior character and integrity and for his ability to govern well and to deal wisely.

Although there are evident the influences of the white man's civilization, the Navajo dress remains distinctive. The men wear a peculiar type of trousers, open on the outside seam at the bottom, often made of a plaid calico and bound at the waist with a bright-colored sash. If it can possibly be afforded the shirt or waist is of a bright-colored velveteen.

Older men wear their hair tied in a knot at the back of the neck with some gaudy material. The younger members of the tribe, particularly those who have been away to school, are beginning to wear their hair "bobbed" straight around at the level of the ear and bound with a gay bandeau. Some now even have it clipped short.

Woman's dress includes a long, heavy, full skirt, sweeping the ground, a tight-fitting bodice of colored velvet, home-made footless socks, and buckskin moccasins or half-boots, dyed red and with silver buttons on the outside seam. Her straight, coal-black hair is tied low at the back of the neck in a sort of club knot. Navajo boys and girls wear clothing identical with that of their elders, except when they are in school.

No Navajo costume would be complete without the profusion of native jewelry worn alike by men, women, and children. Usually the ears of both sexes are pierced and from them hang large turquoise earrings. Invariably there are silver and turquoise bracelets, necklaces of heavy silver, turquoise, shell ornaments, and "wampum." Heavily ornamented leather belts decorated with silver conchos are worn alike by men and women, and very frequently the men wear on their wrists a large silver "kato," originally designed to protect the wrist from the snap of the bow-string. By the amount of jewelry worn, the social standing of a family is judged!

The Navajos are best known to the public for their blankets or rugs. The art of making these is, quite evidently, a comparatively new one among them, for the reason that they had no wool until the introduction of sheep by the Spaniards.

Remnants of cotton fabrics have been found in prehistoric cliff dwellings, and the early Spanish explorers reported that the pueblo Indians were cultivating cotton and weaving it into cloth for garments.

It is generally believed that the Navajos learned weaving from the Hopis, either through capture of Hopi women, or through an agreement by which the Hopis and Zuñis agreed to teach weaving to the Navajos and to exchange blankets and live stock as a guaranty against molestation.

In any event, the Navajo women are most expert weavers of fine rugs or blankets. They prepare the wool by shaking, beating, and picking it, then wash it in a suds made from the root of a yucca known as soapweed, then dye it, until recently making their own vegetable dyes. Formerly they carded the wool with the wild teasel burr, but now they use the wire-toothed card common in Colonial times.

Efforts to introduce the spinning-wheel among the Navajos have been without success. The women use a primitive distaff, about two feet long and thrust through a round wooden disk. The wool is respun sometimes four or five times. It is rare to find a Navajo woman without her wool or her loom.

The value of a Navajo rug depends upon its firmness and smoothness, upon the pattern and its regularity, upon its quality of lying flat upon the floor, and upon the evenness of its edges.

Navajo women rarely lay out a pattern. The artistry of the design is carried in the weaver's head. Rarely does she copy a rug and seldom does she repeat. Among a thousand Navajo rugs, rarely are two found alike.

While the women are working at rugs, the Navajo men are busy with their silver work. Bracelets, earrings, necklaces, conchos, buttons, buckles, rings, and ornamental belts are wrought in large numbers. Often they are set with native stones, notably turquoise. The best of this work is hammered out of silver coins, preferably the Mexican peso, and in spite of the fact that he has but the crudest of tools, the Navajo turns out silver work remarkable for its artistry.

Rugs and silver work are "the bank account" of the Navajo family. Having no permanent home, the Navajo does not care for the luxuries and conveniences of life, other than those which he can carry. Popular demand for rugs and silver work gives him a ready market. In fact, the Navajos are among the most prosperous people of the land.

When a Navajo needs money, he takes a rug or a piece of silverware to a trading post and borrows on it, leaving it in pawn. Sometimes articles are left in pawn for years. The tags on articles in pawn at any trading post are records of the Navajo's financial state, showing amounts borrowed and paid, sometimes over a period of years.

Navajo religious ceremonies take the form of "sings," usually for the healing of the sick. When a Navajo is ill, his friends and relatives for many miles around gather about him to attend these "sings," conducted by the priests or medicine men.

While attending the sing they are guests of the sick man, who must provide food and entertainment for as many as can come, besides paying for the medicine man. Since the sing lasts nine days, it is expensive to be sick.

In most cases, the sing is accompanied by a sand painting on the floor of the hogan. Elaborate designs in many hues are made with colored sands. This is a part of the ceremony for healing the sick. The sand painting is started after sunrise and it is always destroyed before sundown.

In many of the ceremonies the Navajos masquerade as their favorite gods, and while so doing the masquerader may not speak but may gesticulate and utter strange sounds. To all intents and purposes, he is temporarily the god he represents, and as such he hears prayers and accepts sacrifices.

The Navajos are chary of admitting visitors to their hogans or their ceremonies, but if approached properly will occasionally do so. Several Navajos have established their hogans at El Tovar, near the Hopi House, and they weave their rugs and hammer their silverware there before the public.

The Hopi House, used as a studio and curio shop, is an exact duplicate of a typical Hopi house at the Hopi Reservation beyond the Painted Desert. Hopis, in native costume, employed by the curio shop, present their native ceremonial dances daily.

The Hopis belong to the Pueblo group of Indians, so named by the Spanish because they lived in villages. The Hopis are among the most intelligent, artistic, industrious, and peaceful of all American aborigines. The name Hopi (pronounced Hoe-pee) is derived from Hopi-tuh, meaning "the peaceful people."

Just as in 1540, when the Spaniards discovered them, the Hopis still live in villages on three mesas, or table-lands, in the land of the Painted Desert, east of Grand Canyon National Park.

On the easternmost or First Mesa are the villages of Hano, Sichomovi, and Walapai.

On the Second Mesa are Mishnonghovi, Shipaulovi, and Shumopavi.

The westernmost or Third Mesa includes the old village of Oraibi and the more modern communities of Hotevilla and Bacabi. Forty miles northwest is the villlage of Moenkopi, which is the farming center of Oraibi.

Although the residents of these various villages are all of the same tribe and all speak the same language (except that the language of the Tewas is spoken in Hano), the arts and crafts vary on the different mesas.

The people of the First Mesa make no basketry of any kind. Their art is solely one of pottery-making, which has been handed down for generations by the Tewa people, who early in the eighteenth century came from the upper Rio Grande in New Mexico, settling on the First Mesa to join forces with the Hopis against the marauding Utes, Apaches, and Navajos and against the Spaniards. All Hopi pottery comes from the First Mesa, and in the village of Hano live old Nampeyo and her daughter, Kwatsoa, perhaps the most famous of Arizona Indian pottery-makers.

Basketry, but no pottery, is made on the Second and Third Mesas; but there is a very marked difference, readily distinguishable even by the amateur, between the types of baskets and plaques made on these two mesas. The women of the Second Mesa make only basketry of the heavy coil type, while those of the Third Mesa weave wicker baskets and plaques exclusively.

The Hopi male is rather short of stature but exceedingly well muscled and agile. He is a remarkable runner, and in emergencies army officers have preferred a Hopi runner to a man on horseback to carry messages for great distances. The villagers of Oraibi, who worked the fields of Moenkopi, would run to their farms, forty miles distant, put in the day tilling the fields or harvesting their crops, and then run home the forty miles to spend the night. In 1927 Nicholas Quana-wahu, a Hopi of Oraibi, won the Long Beach Marathon of 27 miles and 385 yards from a field of 234 of the best runners of the entire country.

Men wear their straight black hair "bobbed" and bound usually with a single bandeau of brightly colored cloth or ribbon. Their skin is a dark olive brown, cheek bones are fairly high, the mouth is large, and the face is smooth and expressive. The Hopi always has a good-natured smile and a pleasing expression.

The Hopi maidens are quite pretty and even the matrons are comely to behold. However, they age rapidly and one is impressed with the number of wrinkled and bent old gray-headed women to be seen in any Hopi village.

Never have the Hopis gone on the warpath except for purposes of self-defense. Quiet and small of stature, they seek no claim to fame as warriors. The Hopi land is small, entirely surrounded by the Navajo Reservation. From the earliest times the Hopis were preyed upon by the Apaches, Utes, and Navajos. Hence, they banded together in villages, built high on the tops of the mesas overlooking the surrounding desert, to protect themselves better from their enemies.

Hopi-land is truly a land of women's rights. There the husband must live with his wife's relatives. The children belong to the mother, and membership in the various clans into which the tribe is divided is by birth. However, since the mother owns the house and the children, the father is considered only as a sojourner in the clan of his wife, and the children are born into the clan of the mother.

Not only the house but also the corn and other foodstuffs brought into its grain room are the property of the wife. As with the Navajos, she alone has the right of divorce. When the husband returns and finds his belongings set outside the door, he experiences a final decree of divorce. In spite of this tribal law and the ease with which a divorce is accomplished, or perhaps because of it, divorce is comparatively rare and the rule is that husband and wife are faithful, loving, and live happily together, as becomes the Peaceful People.

Except for such income as is had from the sale of basketry and pottery, the Hopis derive their sole livelihood from the products of the soil. Corn is the staple crop and it is grown in a great variety of colors, each having ceremonial significance. One of their legends relates how the prehistoric Kisani brought with them from the lower world an ear of corn for seed and finally agreed to break the ear in half and let the Pueblo people have either end. While they were trying to decide which end to take, the mischievous coyote stole the tip end, leaving for them the butt, which accounts, they say, for the fact that their corn is better than that of other tribes.

Soil and climatic conditions in Hopi-land are extremely unfavorable to agriculture. The desert soil is scant, sandy, and shallow. The Hopi's skill as an agriculturalist is amazing. His efforts meet with success where his white brother would starve.

Since their very existence depends so much upon the necessary amount of rainfall, what could be more natural and logical than that the underlying motive of all the elaborate Hopi ceremonies and tribal dances should be prayers for rain, for bountiful harvests, and for creation of life. These ceremonial dances are more highly developed and more numerous among the Hopis than with any of the other Pueblo tribes. Their nine-day rituals have a fixed order and succeed each other according to the lunar months and the purpose of the ceremony.

Among these are the Soyaluna, or winter solstice ceremony, the Buffalo Dance, the Powamu, or bean-sprouting ceremony, the Kachina dances, the Basket dances, the New Fire ceremony, and others.

The Snake and Antelope ceremony, commonly known as the Snake Dance, is the ritual of which the outside world hears most. This is given jointly by the Antelope and the Snake clans and, in common with many others, it is a nine-day ceremonial solely with reference to rain-bringing. The date of the ceremonial is determined by the priests of the clan from certain phases of the moon; generally, it is about the middle of August.

The Indians do not worship or make their prayers directly to the snakes. The snakes are merely messengers to carry prayers to the rain gods and to the Great Plumed Water Serpent, all of whom live in the Underworld. If the snakes are well treated by being danced over, sprinkled with sacred meal, washed and bathed during these elaborate ceremonies, the Hopi reasons that they will most certainly return all these courtesies by asking their friends, the rain gods, to send rain. White men who are caught frequently in desert storms and cloudbursts on their way home from the Snake Dance ceremonial testify to the efficiency of the snakes as messengers.

In preparation for the ceremonial, the snake priests go

out in pairs in the four directions of the compass to collect from over the desert the required number of snakes, usually from sixty to eighty, at least half of which must be rattlesnakes.

The snakes are taken into the kivas or ceremonial chambers, where secret rites are conducted of which there is little authentic information. It is known that altars are erected by each clan in its own kiva, that many prayers are uttered, dances are performed, and chants of great antiquity are sung, that there is much ceremonial smoking of native tobacco, and that the snakes are bathed and carefully sprinkled many times with sacred corn meal.

At the termination of these secret underground ceremonies and as a sort of grand finale the snakes are brought out into the open where the final dance is performed. This is the only part of the nine-day ceremony which may be seen by white men, and at its conclusion the runners again go down from the mesa and out upon the desert to the four cardinal directions, this time carrying with them handfuls of snakes, which are turned loose to carry their messages to their underground homes.

Hopi boys are trained from very early childhood in the mysteries of the Snake Dance. Youngsters of four and five years of age take part in the ceremonies, handling the rattlesnakes with the same fearlessness as their elders. These boys are younger members of the Snake and Antelope clans who will eventually become priests.

"Why don't the snakes bite the dancers?" visitors always ask.

It can be seen during the dance that the rattlesnakes do frequently strike the performers. It is also known for a certainty that fangs and poison sacs have not been removed. It must be remembered, however, that during the nine-day ceremonial the snakes have been handled continuously and perhaps partially tamed. Also that the sacred meal, with which they have been frequently sprinkled, partially blinds their lidless eyes. Through long years of experience the priests have become very skillful in warding off attacks. It is quite probable that during the nine-day secret rites and just before the snakes are brought out into the open, they have been teased and made to strike at sticks or cloths until their venom has been partially exhausted.

The Hopis have their medicine women as well as their medicine men. Chief among these are the mothers of the snake priests, and it is definitely known that they have a formula for a snake-poison antidote, the secret of which is most carefully guarded and passed down from generation to generation. The dancers not only wash themselves with this preparation, but they also take it internally, and when so used it acts very promptly and powerfully as an emetic.

The Hopi Snake Dance is the most peculiar and interesting ceremony conducted by any American Indians. It is one of the most sacred of the Hopi ceremonials, one well worth going long distances to see. Visitors should regard it as sacred and not look upon it as a show for their entertainment.

Hopi-land can be reached in one day by motor from the Grand Canyon and any traveler who can do so should attend a Snake Dance.

Photo by Homer S. Jones

Deer in the Kaibab Forest

Photo by Willard S. Wood

Quaking aspens and meadow in the Kaibab Forest

El Tovar Studio

The Colorado River and wall of inner gorge

IV. THE STORY OF THE PARK

It was a curious circumstance that, though the Grand Canyon was the first of the great American natural wonders to be discovered, it was one of the last to be preserved as a national park from private exploitation.

Back in 1886, Benjamin Harrison, then a United States Senator from Indiana, introduced a bill to make the Grand Canyon a national park. From that time on it was the plaything of politics, as conflicting interests struggled to control the territory now in the park for local or private advantage.

The obstacles to the creation of Grand Canyon National Park were more numerous than those encountered in any other national playland.

Hunters, in the early days, opposed the idea of a park because it would cut off one of their important sources of supply for beaver pelts. Beaver trapping in the side canyons was an industry. Once a railroad route was surveyed through the Grand Canyon, at the behest of Eastern capitalists, but the project never reached the point of actual construction. Gold in small quantities was found in the canyon walls, and certain copper and asbestos claims were located. Consequently, numerous mining claims were staked out in the area, and were granted before the park area was reserved. These claims were declared invalid later by the Government, but it was only after long litigation ending in the United States Supreme Court that the holders were eliminated. Cattle and sheep men once grazed thousands of animals along both rims of the Canyon. They opposed the creation of a park which would cut off their pasturage.

Water-power sites were in demand by big companies along the turbulent river. In fact, during the year that the park was created, an attempt was made in New York to raise money to dam the river for power and irrigation purposes. Passage in 1928 of a bill authorizing the project at Boulder Dam, well outside the park, ended this menace to the Canyon.

In the early days, trails into the Canyon were constructed by private parties, to reach mining claims, or for the purpose of conducting tourists into the Canyon. These owners were not only reluctant to give up their holdings, but were likewise active in resisting the movement for creation of the park.

They resorted frequently to political sabotage. Grand Canyon National Park lies entirely in one county, Coconino, the largest and most sparsely settled in Arizona. Politicians contended that removal of so many acres from their tax rolls to the public domain would impoverish the county.

The first withdrawal or reservation of any kind was made in 1893, when on February 20, Benjamin Harrison, by that time President of the United States, created the Grand Canyon Forest Reserve by proclamation.

This reserve was twice enlarged and was eventually divided into three national forests known as Kaibab, Tusayan, and Coconino. Grand Canyon lay entirely within these national forests.

That status failed to protect it from private exploitation,

inasmuch as the law authorized the granting of mining and other claims within national forests. It did enable federal officials to maintain some protection over the area, however, and to control squatters.

Meantime, agitation for the creation of a national park was persistent, but efforts were frustrated by politics, local apathy, and private interests. President Roosevelt finally became alarmed at the inroads of private enterprise and on January 11, 1908, by executive order, created the Grand Canyon National Monument.

It remained under the administration of the National Forest Service until February 26, 1919, when the Grand Canyon National Park was created by an act of Congress drafted by Senator Ashurst and Congressman (now Senator) Hayden and turned over to the National Park Service of the Department of the Interior.

Since that date, the National Park Service has sought to rid the park of private holdings. The Park Service has been successful in securing the privately owned Bright Angel Trail, but there are still a number of private holdings along the rim. Recently, Congressional authority was granted for condemnation of private holdings, but sufficient funds for their purchase under such proceedings were not provided at that time.

The total area of Grand Canyon National Park is 1,009 square miles, or approximately 645,000 acres. The air-line length from west to east is approximately 56 miles, and through it winds the Colorado River for a distance of 105 miles. The eastern boundary includes the lofty colorful walls beyond which lies the Painted Desert, and runs along the east base of Cedar Mountain, the flat-topped butte which may be seen two or three miles to the east of Desert View. Its western boundaries include the watershed of the beautiful Havasu Canyon.

Grand Canyon National Park includes both the North and the South Rims. However, the boundaries of the park include but a very little of the country back of the rims. With the rapid increase in travel and consequent greater use of the park, the need for additional area is already being felt. For the adequate protection of the wild life with which the park abounds there must be an extension of the park boundaries, particularly on the North Rim where roam the great herds of Kaibab mule deer.

Grand Canyon is one of the twenty-one parks under the jurisdiction of the Director of the National Park Service of the Department of the Interior. The act of Congress creating this Service declared the purpose of a national park to be as follows: "To conserve the scenery and the natural and historic objects and the wild life therein, and to provide for the enjoyment of the same in such manner and by such means as will leave them unimpaired for the enjoyment of future generations."

No effort is made to beautify the parks as city parks are developed. In fact, quite the opposite is the plan, and landscape architects are employed to see that any roadway or other construction in the national park does not infringe on the natural beauty of the wilderness.

The officer immediately in charge of the park is the Superintendent, whose offices are located at the South Rim of Grand Canyon. He is aided by an assistant superintendent, park engineer, clerks, accountants, and a staff of rangers, stationed at various points in the park area.

In a national park of the type of Grand Canyon, there are thousands of visitors who want to ask questions about the natural wonders. Answering questions is one of the best things that the rangers do.

In recent years the National Park Service has not contented itself with merely answering inquiries—it has arranged actively to educate people who are interested in the wonders of their national parks. The educational staff in each park includes a group of ranger-naturalists, trained in the lore of the region, who conduct walking trips, lecture to visitors, and maintain a museum in which are exhibits illustrating the scientific wonders of the park.

The range of questions which the rangers and naturalists are called upon to answer is as wide and as wonderful as the Grand Canyon itself. Here is just a sample of them:

"Ranger, how far is the river below sea-level?"

How a river can be expected to flow uphill to sea-level is more than the rangers can figure out, but they must answer with a straight face.

A party had made camp on the South Rim for the night when a nervous mother approached a ranger and asked:

"Oh, Ranger, is there any danger that the river might overflow and wet our camp?"

The engineer who had just spent $150,000 and three years blasting rock and building the Kaibab Trail, a regular "boulevard" down into the Canyon, was asked:

"Who discovered this wonderful natural trail down the mountain side?"

In one of Zane Grey's stories, *Wildfire,* the leader of a band of wild horses is chased across the Canyon and finally captured. An amazing number of Zane Grey enthusiasts are concerned with but one thought, as they gaze across the Canyon the first time.

"How in blazes could they chase Wildfire across there?" they ask.

Nina Wilcox Putnam, in *West of Broadway,* tells so vividly of her ride down the Canyon trails on a mule called "Napoleon" that scores of visitors want to see this famous mule.

"Where's Napoleon?" they ask.

"That's him," says the guide, pointing to the nearest mule.

"Oh, I want to ride Napoleon."

"Hol' still, Napoleon. Get right on, ma'am."

Which explains why "Napoleon" is the name of every other mule in the park. Sometimes "Napoleon" is black, sometimes white, sometimes masculine, frequently feminine. Good old "Napoleon!"

A famous engineer visited the park, walked up to the rim, inquired the depth and the width and the length of the Canyon. He gazed in silence at the sea of silent pastels, then said:

"Well, it's a hell of a big hole, but what'll you bet I can't fill her up for a dollar a cubic yard?"

An important part of a ranger's job is knowing what not to say. We have mentioned already the danger of incurring the ire of people who take the Bible story of creation entirely literally.

Recently a ranger overheard a woman pointing out to her companions a dry wash in a side canyon. She thought this was the Colorado River. The ranger stepped up politely and said:

"I beg your pardon, ma'am, but that is Trinity Wash, and it is dry at this time of year. The Colorado River is not visible at this point.

The woman drew herself up haughtily.

"I know better," she declared. "My cousin was here three years ago and he said he could see the river from here. I will take my cousin's word for it any time to that of a perfect stranger!"

It can be seen readily that the rangers must be a patient and resourceful body of men. Of course, not all visitors ask foolish questions—"at least, not all the time," as one ranger put it.

The ranger regards it as the most important part of his business to see that "dudes," the visitors who arrive on trains, and "sagebrushers," those who drive their own cars, learn all about the park and get the most possible out of their all-too-fleeting visits.

During the season, the ranger spends most of his time rendering little courtesies to visitors. In his odd moments, and after everyone else has gone to bed, he may find time to attend to his regular duties of running the park.

A national park, notwithstanding all our efforts to keep Nature natural, is a complicated affair. It just can't be otherwise, with a quarter of a million people or more visiting it each year. A quarter of a million people need a lot of water to drink, and much more to bathe in and to fill their radiators. There is no water at either rim, owing to the peculiar geologic formation of the area. Nevertheless, at either North or South Rim, all the camper or the hotel guest has to do is turn the faucet, and water flows out, just as it does at home.

This is made possible by hauling a train load of water in tank cars on the Santa Fe daily from springs one hundred miles away to the South Rim and pumping it into a high tank. On the North Rim, the water is boosted from Roaring Springs, half-way down the Canyon, by some of the most remarkable hydroelectric projects known, a part of the Union Pacific development of Grand Canyon Lodge.

With water so scarce and costly, the problem of sewage disposal is an acute one. The sanitary system, by which all water is purified and reclaimed for use in boilers and for watering, is one which sanitary engineers come to inspect from all over the country.

A national park, in spite of its isolation in a wilderness, is a small city, with all the problems of a community. The difference is that the Superintendent is the more or less autocratic manager of the community, subject, of course, to orders from his employer, the United States Government, and he can work out community problems without the delay of local politics.

The Superintendent is the chief officer to maintain peace and order, in co-operation with county and state authorities. He is responsible for the water supply, the sanitary system and the communication service. He must know road building and trail construction, and in addition is head of a museum, with a staff maintained to educate visitors, most of them adults.

The Superintendent must have an eye to landscaping, and not permit construction to damage beautiful views. He must be an amateur at least at natural science and must protect not only wild animals but wild flowers. He must know how to stock streams with fish, and must be equally at home entertaining Presidents, Kings, Senators, or commoners, for everyone sooner or later comes to Grand Canyon.

Not only that, but he must have a flair for diplomacy and must maintain friendly relations with local state and county officials, who are not always enthusiastic about having jurisdiction of park area in the hands of an outsider, a federal appointee. There are plenty of other duties, such as maintaining roads and trails, collecting entrance fees, making speeches at dedications, et cetera, but these are enough to indicate that a park superintendent finds plenty to do.

When everything has been attended to and the forest fires which lightning has started have all been put out, and the trout eggs are incubating in Ribbon Creek after a forty-mile ride across the desert and the trails on mule back, the Superintendent can go home to his wife and children in the little log cabin with the crackling fire and there isn't anything to do until tomorrow—unless the telephone rings.

Then, like as not, the voice on the wire, from a town a hundred miles away, may say:

"Listen, Ranger——" (Everybody in the National Park Service uniform, from the Director down, is a ranger to the public.)

"There's a party of four Oklahoma bank robbers, armed with plenty of artillery, headed for the park. Try and catch them before they get hidden in the Canyon, will you."

Under the circumstances, there is nothing to do but round up a dozen or so rangers and go out and catch the bandits. Fortunately, the record for catching fugitives from justice is so near one hundred per cent in the national parks that not many of them try to slip past the rangers.

The air of peaceful tranquillity at a national park is due not alone to Nature. When several thousand visitors have gathered at one time at one spot, even the wilderness may at times seem a bit hectic. It is then that the work of the rangers becomes most important. Quietly, and without anybody noticing it, the rangers see that the campers are scattered out so that they are not too crowded, that firewood is available, and that everybody is happy, according to fifty-seven varieties of ideas concerning what constitutes happiness.

These national parks rangers are a remarkable body of men. The regulars, or old-timers, are for the most part men who have not been able to resist the call of the wilderness. They have lived most of their days "a stone's throw from Nature." They love their work as rangers because it gives them the maximum of time on the trails. Their training has made them at home in the wilds and equal to emergencies as they arise.

For courage, resourcefulness, and devotion to duty, it is hard to find a finer group of men than those who have appeared at the national parks to serve as rangers. Their hours are long, their duties hard, their wages low, yet their morale as an organization is equaled only by that of such outfits as the Canadian Mounted Police.

Chief Ranger Jim Brooks, at Grand Canyon, is typical of the finest type of national park ranger. For courage, initiative, resourcefulness, stamina, and knowledge of both wild life and human nature, it is hard to find his equal.

His headquarters are at South Rim, but he is often found at North Rim where Art Brown, Assistant Chief Ranger, holds forth.

The true park ranger is not only an officer of the Government, but he is also a friend and confidant of the visitor in the park. Everybody likes to "talk things over" with a ranger. The ranger must know intuitively how to be a friend of prince or pauper, industrial potentate, or his son's school-teacher. Every citizen knows that he owns a share in the national park. When he visits a park he expects the rangers to treat him as though he were a long-absent owner returned to his estate.

During the summer seasons, when travel is heaviest, the handful of regular rangers on duty is so small in numbers that they must be augmented by the "ninety-day wonders," or temporary rangers. These lads are mostly college boys, working during their vacations. Eager to learn, they are put through an intensive course in woodcraft and public service and are then assigned as assistants to the regular rangers.

This is wonderful training for a college youngster. He may be fighting forest fires one minute, planting fish the next, directing "sagebrushers" to camp-sites the following; then he may run the whole gamut of ranger duties, registration of motorists, protection of wild life, marking trails, rescuing hikers lost on the trails—known in ranger vernacular as "making a drag-out"—or repairing a telephone line, or what will you?

During the winter season, when the North Rim of Grand Canyon is shut off from civilization by more than a hundred miles of impassable snows, it is the duty of the rangers to patrol this winter-bound wilderness, mainly for the protection of the wild life, the property of the Government, and the operators of concessions.

In the winter months, the snows pile up to a depth of six feet or more all along the North Rim. The rangers assigned to this area make their headquarters near Grand Canyon Lodge, but their duties include long patrols on snowshoes to check up on game and forest conditions and to maintain telephone lines.

At this time of year, the north slope of the Grand Canyon offers the widest imaginable range of climatic conditions. A ranger may turn his snowshoes to the north and face mile after mile of almost impenetrable wilderness in the grip of Arctic winter. Or he may discard snowshoes, head down the Kaibab Trail afoot or on horseback and within an hour or two find himself in almost tropical warmth, surrounded by brilliantly colored desert flowers.

"It's all in the day's work," says the ranger, with a shrug. He is ready for anything.

Finally, there is the duty of seeing that the operators of concessions, such as hotels, camps, stores, garages, and transportation lines, render good service at reasonable rates to the visiting public.

The Act of Congress creating the National Parks authorized that facilities for enjoying these wildernesses must be provided. Since it was contrary to the prevailing American idea for the Government to be in business which private capital could develop equally well, the matter of lodging, feeding, transporting, and supplying the public was granted to private concessioners.

All concessions are under the strict control of the Secretary of the Interior, however, and he determines what services must be rendered and regulates the rates. The superintendent of the park and his assistants are the agents of the federal government to see that services are rendered and that rates are prescribed.

Each park presents its own peculiar set of administrative problems. Conditions of travel, terrain, proximity to or distance from centers of population, and natural conditions determine what they are.

For example, Grand Canyon is the only park into which a railroad has been built. Travelers may reach the South Rim in Pullman coaches the year around. It is the only park without a water supply near the resort centers. The very nature of the Canyon, isolating the two rims except by thirty miles of trail or two hundred miles of road, presents a problem. South Rim is an all-year travel center. The North Rim is visited only during a summer season, which opens with a rush and ends almost as abruptly.

Grand Canyon has been called the "two-in-one park," on account of the widely different conditions found on the two rims. The range of interesting problems presented by Grand Canyon makes it a fascinating place, even to the man who has spent much of his life there—yes, even to the Superintendent who must be able to spread himself out exceedingly thin at times.

As the chief clerk remarked to a visitor who asked where the Superintendent held forth:

"Well, he spends some time on the South Rim and he spends some more time on the North Rim, but most of the time he spends in the saddle of a mule somewhere on the trail in between."

V. MAKING THE WILDERNESS EASY TO ENJOY

Just as soon as a region of natural wonders is set aside as a national park, the administrators of that area find themselves between millstones of public opinion.

One group, largely motorists, wants highways built into the wilderness immediately.

Another group, the Nature lovers, opposes any further road-building into the few remaining wilderness areas.

"What's the use of a national park if the public can't enjoy it easily?" demands the motorist.

"How long will it remain a wilderness, if you criss-cross it with highways?" asks the Nature lover, in reply.

Every national park has its own particular "battle line," so to speak. In Grand Canyon National Park, the great issue has been the project of a road across the Canyon by which motorists could descend to the river and ascend the opposite rim. At present the trip from rim to rim can be made only by way of the Kaibab Trail afoot or on mule back, or by a two-hundred-and-forty-mile trip via Lee's Ferry Bridge.

From an engineering standpoint a road from rim to rim is entirely feasible, albeit costly.

"Give me enough money, and I can fill the Grand Canyon," remarked a famous engineer.

It would take a lot; so would a highway from rim to rim, particularly if it were built so as to avoid despoliation of the landscape. In a chasm as huge as the Grand Canyon, a road would be but a thread, hardly visible.

The National Park Service is strongly opposed to this project, however. It feels that a highway across the park would destroy the majesty of the Grand Canyon.

To break the age-long silence of the Canyon with the honking of horns, to carve roadways into its formidable rainbow walls, to impair the normal impregnability of Nature, to make it easy for anyone to conquer the Grand Canyon, that would be sacrilegious indeed.

Yet the proponents of the Rim-to-Rim road are active, and every so often we read in the Arizona newspapers headlines like these:

"Superintendent Plans Highway Across Grand Canyon."

This is a good place, perhaps, for the Superintendent to put himself on record. He is opposed to the Rim-to-Rim Highway, but if it must be built, in response to public demand, he wants to be the engineer to do it.

What engineer wouldn't? Eleven miles to go, as the crow flies! A mile down to the river and a mile back up again! A bridge to defy the turbulent Colorado! Cliffs that have defied both man and beast, to be conquered by compressed air, powder, and steam shovels! A brand new problem at every turn, and thousands of turns in the road! What engineer wouldn't give his eye-teeth to be in charge of that job, if it ever develops—and here's hoping it never does.

When Congress created the national parks, the act specified the preservation of natural wonders, without despoliation, but also authorized the National Park Service to provide necessary roads and trails and other facilities, so that these wonders might be enjoyed easily by the public.

"Congress ordered the parks preserved as wildernesses and game refuges," the Nature lovers contend, after reading the law.

"But Congress ordered roads built and provided money for them," retorts the motorist.

Both sides are right. The National Park Service, in the past ten years, has spent millions of dollars building roads, but practically all of this money has gone to improve old roads that have been in use for years, to bring them up to standard for automobile travel. Practically every park area was crossed by roads and trails before it became a park. In many cases the roads were mere scratches in the earth, improved only by occasional dragging. Often the road was but an old trail, widened so that horse-drawn vehicles might pass over it precariously during the summer months.

The evolution of a road, before the automobile made highway-building a science, is a fascinating study. First came the trail, pounded by the countless hoofs of wild animals, in their migrations for forage. The animals found the faults along the mountain cliffs. They invariably took the easiest route between points. Next came the Indian. He, too, took the easiest way, and generally followed the trails of the wild animals, or followed geologic faults. Only a few of the Southwestern Indians made any effort to construct trails, and these were but paths to their cliff dwellings.

The early explorers, hunters, trappers, and traders followed the Indian, as much as possible, because they used Indian guides, and also because the old routes were the easiest to follow. These pioneers widened and improved the narrow paths so that packhorses might use them.

Fred Harvey Photo

A sea of clouds fills the Canyon

El Tovar Studio

On the Tonto Plateau

Courtesy Santa Fe Railway

Kaibab Trail, carved in the walls of the Canyon

Next came the buckboard of the early settlers. All that was required to change the trail into a road was width, and not very much of that. Of course, there were many trails along the cliffs, that could never become roads.

After the buckboard came the stage coach, which swayed and rolled and rollicked over the roughest of roads and over grades that would make the motorist cringe. Those were the days when the dude got his money's worth in hair-raising thrills.

It was not until 1913 that automobiles were permitted in the national parks. Even then the federal authorities stated, in a report, that the automobile would never come into general use in the parks areas. If anyone had suggested then that within fifteen years motorists would be arriving in the parks three million strong each year, or that motorists would be demanding a road over which to drive into the Grand Canyon, his hallucinations would have been credited to the heat or the altitude.

The automobile era ushered in a period of road-building in all of the national parks, accompanied by an extensive trail-construction program, so that thousands of visitors might scatter through the park areas and each have unto himself all the wilderness he could enjoy.

Older members of the Havasupai tribe still living in the Canyon tell how in their younger days they traveled regularly along the great geologic fault which is now the scientifically chosen route of the Bright Angel Trail. Thus instinct led the savage over the very route laid out later by the surveyor's transit.

"Big Jim," one of the Havasupais, a picturesque character who wears an official decoration from King Albert of the Belgians, along with a fine assortment of convention badges and medals, whenever he leaves the reservation, still remembers the primitive trails of the Canyon.

"Big Jim" was born at Indian Gardens, on the present Bright Angel Trail. When but a small boy, his people learned, by the mysterious Indian underground telegraph system, of a new tribe of strange people with white skins who had settled at a place near where Prescott is now located.

With his parents, Jim, then a small Indian boy, journeyed along the Bright Angel fault to the rim and followed the trail across the plateau for many miles, solely for the purpose of seeing these strange pale-faces. Their curiosity satisfied, Jim says the three retraced their steps back down the trail to their isolated home.

The Spaniards under Cardenas, who reached the South Rim in 1540, evidently did not find any of these old Indian trails, or their lust and curiosity would have led them down to the then numerous Havasupai settlements along the river.

As stated in an earlier chapter, in 1776 the exploring padres, Garces and Escalante, seeking a route to Monterey, discovered the Indian trail into Havasu Canyon. They followed it, visited the Indians, and crossed the river at the ford used by the Utes in their migrations, afterward known as the "Crossing of the Padres." The padres were not impressed with these rough, natural trails.

Although numerous pathfinders, hunters, and trappers penetrated the Canyon during the early part of the nineteenth century, sturdy Mormon colonists sent out by Brigham Young to develop and populate the arid Southwest were responsible for the first improvement of Grand Canyon trails.

Brigham Young and his followers dreamed of a vast independent empire, to be known as the State of Deseret, extending from Colorado to the Gulf of California. The Grand Canyon cut across the heart of it and was one of the obstacles which the great Mormon leader failed to overcome in the realization of his spectacular dream.

Jacob Hamblin, the Mormon frontiersman and missionary extraordinary, first explored the Canyon from the North Rim, seeking crossings. Hamblin and his associates improved several of the old Indian trails and made frequent crossings.

The first maintained trails into the Canyon were those of the gold prospectors and miners. By the early 'eighties, at least five trails, Tanner, Hance, Red Canyon, Grand View, and Bass, led from the rim to the river. According to modern standards, they were mere scratches along the Canyon walls, but they were at least passable to the hardy and the wary.

Hance Trail, an improved Indian path, was used by the first white woman to penetrate the Canyon. She was Mrs. Edward Ayres, wife of a pioneer Flagstaff sawmill man. Her memorable trip was in February 1882.

Grand View Trail was constructed by P. D. ("Pete") Berry and associates interested in reaching certain copper claims on Horseshoe Mesa.

The first Government trail was undertaken in 1882 to provide a route over which men and supplies might be transported to make geological surveys. The route led from North Rim via House Rock Valley and Nankoweap Creek.

Major J. H. Powell, who first traversed the Canyon by boat, directed this work.

In 1911–1912, the Santa Fe Railway Company constructed the Hermit Trail from a point on the South Rim seven miles south of El Tovar, to Hermit Creek, near the River, where was located the first resort in the Canyon, Hermit Camp. This privately owned trail was turned over to the National Park Service in 1919, when the Grand Canyon country became a national park.

Undoubtedly, the most famous trail in Grand Canyon is the Bright Angel. Starting at El Tovar, it follows the route of the Old Indian Trail to Indian Gardens, along the Bright Angel geologic fault. The trail was developed for modern use in 1890–1891 by a group headed by "Pete" Berry.

For many years Bright Angel Trail constituted a park problem. Improved by private owners, it became the property of Coconino County in the course of a tangled political deal, and the county officials charged toll for the use of it. This was contrary to the national park policy, and it was only after protracted negotiations that Bright Angel Trail became public property.

Toll charges were discontinued, of course, and in June 1928 this oldest and most widely known route, so rich in scenic interest, was taken over by the National Park Service. This was a great victory for the park, since it put an end to privately owned toll ways in the parks.

The Bright Angel is the "one-day trip" to the river for those who have no longer time at the Canyon. Halfway down are the cool and shaded Indian Gardens, where the Havasupais cultivated their little farms in early days. The trail is visible from South Rim for much of the way, and one of the favorite pastimes of visitors is "spotting trail parties" far below.

Kaibab Trail, the newest and best trail in the park, is the only trans-canyon trail. Starting at Yaki Point, three and one-half miles east of El Tovar, it winds down the South Rim walls to the River and to Phantom Ranch, then follows Bright Angel Canyon up the North Rim slope to a point near Grand Canyon Lodge, a total distance of twenty and one-half miles.

Kaibab Trail is the last word in modern trail-building. Its construction has been called "one of the engineering romances of the West." Certainly, it presented plenty of problems during the building, but the result is, as someone said, "a trail down which you could ride a motorcycle." Kaibab Trail is wide, has easy grades, and is banked by rock guard-walls wherever it winds along precipitous cliffs, so that even the most timid trail rider need have no apprehensions. Some high spots in this "romance of engineering" are these:

The route was selected only after a long series of preliminary surveys by engineers, because the entire route, except for a quarter of a mile, is reached by the sun's rays. Thus the trail could be kept free of snow and passable the year around. This was an important factor, since the Kaibab is the only connection between the two rims during much of the year. The route utilizes a series of ridges on the South Rim slope. Thus it has natural drainage and is free from snowslides.

Construction was both daring and ingenious. Almost every foot of the way was blasted out of the solid rock of the Canyon walls. Air compressors, jack-hammers, other machinery, gas, oil, tents, food, and many tons of explosives were packed down into the Canyon on mule back. At some camp-sites, even wood and water were packed down on mules.

The trail crosses the Colorado over the new Kaibab suspension bridge, three-quarters of a mile from Phantom Ranch, near the mouth of Bright Angel Creek. From there it winds for eight miles along this clear and beautiful mountain stream, named by Major Powell "The Bright Angel" in 1869 in contrast to a particularly muddy stream now known as Fremont River, which he had discovered some time previously and had called "The Dirty Devil."

Five and one-half miles above Phantom Ranch is Ribbon Falls, where a small, clear tributary to Bright Angel Creek forms a beautiful ribbon-like waterfall 148 feet in height. The lime-impregnated waters of Ribbon Creek have piled up a large stalagmite or "altar" of travertine at the base of the falls. This altar, 42 feet high, covered with an emerald green moss and with its setting among the colorful rock walls of the Canyon, a rainbow continually playing at the base of the falls in the sunlight, makes one of the most entrancing sights to be found anywhere in the Park.

Continuing upward, the Kaibab Trail is almost continually in sight of prehistoric cliff dwellings, food caches, mescal pits, and other evidences of a prehistoric life. Beaver cuttings, new and old, may be seen on every hand, and the dams built by these interesting and industrious little animals are occasionally found, although it is very rare that one is so fortunate as to see a beaver at work.

At Cottonwood Flat a stop may be made for rest under the shade of a grove of large cottonwood trees. Here from the east a large side canyon joins Bright Angel Creek. This is known as The Transept, from its fancied resemblance to the cross-aisle of a cathedral, coming in as it does at almost an exact right angle to the main stream or "nave."

At the mouth of Manzanita Creek is located the unique hydroelectric plant, which furnishes power for pumping water to supply the North Rim. Here Roaring Springs gush forth with a rush from beneath the red-wall limestone and cascade in three large streams down the oak-covered mountainside to the bottom of the side canyon 400 feet below. This offers one of the most spectacular views of the Grand Canyon.

Through the red-wall limestone above Roaring Springs, the construction of the Kaibab Trail was particularly difficult and daring. Here the trail was literally hewn from the solid rock cliff in half-tunnel sections. At such points, however, there is a heavy rock guard-wall of such proportions that the traveler has no feeling of insecurity.

At one point in the red sandstone of the Supai formation the trail passes through a thirty-eight-foot tunnel, above which the scene changes entirely and the traveler at once enters the heavy oak and locust brush characteristic of North Rim Canyon slopes. Soon there are encountered the yellow pines, then the Douglas firs, and finally the quaking aspen of the higher altitudes; and the Kaibab Trail finally "tops out" on Bright Angel Point at an elevation of 8,350 feet.

Construction work on the Kaibab Trail started in December 1924. It was finally completed all the way to the

North Rim in May 1928. However, work was not continuous between those dates. For the most part, construction work was carried on only during the winter months and the crews were transferred to road work on the rims during the summer. The total cost, rim to rim, was approximately $146,000, exclusive of the Kaibab Suspension Bridge, which added $39,500.

Before the Kaibab Trail was built there was a route or so-called trail by which the North Rim could be reached. This was via the Bright Angel Trail to the Tonto Plateau, thence along the Tonto Trail to the Tip-Off and down an old trail, extremely steep and rough, to the river. Up Bright Angel Creek this old trail followed approximately the route of the present Kaibab Trail as far as Manzanita Creek, but it crossed and recrossed Bright Angel Creek ninety-four times, each ford being extremely rough and strewn with large boulders. Crossings were difficult and even dangerous. By the new trail there are just seven crossings.

Until 1921 the only means of crossing the Colorado River in the Park was by swimming or by an old cableway near the mouth of Bright Angel Creek. During that year, however, the Park Service constructed a light "swinging" bridge, which served the purpose until it was replaced in 1928 with a more modern and rigid structural steel suspension bridge.

This new bridge is suspended from eight steel cables, each one and one-half inches in diameter; the steel floor is paved with asphalt, and the structural steel members were designed and fabricated especially for transportation from the rim to the bottom of the Canyon on the backs of pack mules.

Since the total amount of structural steel that went into the construction of this bridge amounted to some sixty-seven tons, and since additional material, such as cement, camp supplies, and equipment, made the grand total approximately 122 tons, it can readily be appreciated that it was no small job to pack all this from the rim to the bottom of the Canyon by mule back.

This super-packing job was handled by Jack Way, Park Service packmaster, than whom a better packer never pulled a lash rope. Something as to Jack Way's ability as a packer may be judged from the fact that on this entire job he never lost or injured an animal, there was never a mule with a sore back, and at the time the job was finished, the mules were actually in better condition than at the start.

In addition to the eight suspension cables, there were two one-and-one-half-inch wind cables, making ten in all. These cables were 548 feet in length, and weighed 2,030 pounds each. Obviously they could not be packed on mule back!

They were, therefore, transported to the river by man power. The cables were unreeled and laid on the ground at the rim. A gang of fifty men, mostly Indians, were then lined up alongside the strung-out cable. Two men were placed at each end and the rest were strung out from ten to twelve feet apart. At a given signal the men stooped over, picked up the cable, placed it on their shoulders, and started the long march of six and one-half miles down the Kaibab Trail to the bridge site.

Ten such round trips were necessary before the cables were on the job ready to be put in place. It was most interesting to see these great cables being taken down the trail and around the many switchbacks. From a distance it looked like some gigantic centipede.

The bridge is four hundred and forty feet long, five feet wide, and about sixty-five feet above the river. The south approach to the bridge is through 105 feet of tunnel cut in the solid granite.

The next bridge down stream from the Kaibab Suspension bridge is the one at Topock, Arizona, a distance of 385 miles away. Upstream the nearest bridge was, at the time the Kaibab Bridge was completed, at Moab, Utah, a distance of 370 miles, making a total distance of 755 miles of river spanned by but this one bridge. There was probably no other bridge in the United States which served so long a stretch of a stream as large and important as the Colorado River.

Since the Kaibab Bridge was completed, however, the new Lee's Ferry Highway Bridge has been constructed and opened to traffic, eighty-six miles upstream via the river. The distance by auto road from Grand Canyon to the Lee's Ferry Bridge is approximately 140 miles.

Extending along the Tonto Plateau on the south side of the river is a trail known as the Tonto Trail, connecting the Hermit, Bright Angel, and Kaibab Trails. The Tonto Trail is comparatively level, and over it "loop trips" may be arranged. For example, one may go down the Hermit, across the Tonto, and up the Bright Angel or Kaibab Trails. In many places the Tonto Trail extends along the very rim of the so-called Granite Gorge, affording a most spectacular trip almost directly above the river. It crosses Monument, Salt, Horn, Garden, and Pipe Creeks, each of which flows in a canyon that would be considered a marvel in itself, were it not dwarfed by the immensity of the Grand Canyon.

On both rims foot and bridle paths along the Canyon rim and into the beautiful back country have been laid out.

In both directions from El Tovar hotel on the South Rim, paved footpaths follow closely the contour of the rim eastward via Grandeur Point to the museum or observation station at Yavapai Point and westward to Powell Memorial Point.

Extending from the camp ground on the North Rim an excellent footpath entirely encircles Grand Canyon Lodge and extends out to the extreme end of Bright Angel Point.

At North Rim, bridle paths have been constructed to McKinnon and Natchi Points, to Farview, Point Imperial, and many similar scenes of unusual interest. These trails lead through heavily timbered sections interrupted by many open park-like glades, free from underbrush and plentiful in wild animal life. The way to see Nature at her best and at close range is afoot or from the saddle.

Among the older Canyon trails, there should be mentioned the Topocoba, which extends from Hilltop, some thirty-five miles west of Grand Canyon Village on the South Rim, down Lee Canyon to Havasu or Cataract Canyon, and thence to the Havasupai Indian Reservation. Even the Havasupai Indians know nothing as to the origin of this trail. The oldest member of the tribe has no recollection of the time when this trail was not in use. Down it, in earlier days, came the Apaches on their expeditions to raid the stores of corn and other foodstuffs harvested by the Havasupai Indians.

This trail is still in continuous use by the Indians and by such white men as visit their homes. It is a regular United States Mail route between the postoffices of Grand Canyon and Supai. The Indian mail-carrier hauls the mail pouches by auto from Grand Canyon to Hilltop, and thence by pack horse down this fourteen-mile stretch of exceedingly poor trail to the agency.

Along the trail at the junction of Lee and Havasu Canyons are large numbers of exceedingly clear and well-preserved Indian hieroglyphics. The modern Supai has no recollection or knowledge of the origin of these pictographs. One interesting feature about them is the fact that they plainly portray in several places an animal with long straight horns extending well over the back. These are what might be expected of an inexperienced or amateur artist attempting to picture an ibex, and it is a well-known fact that Indian pictographs portray only those objects of everyday life with which these early artists were familiar. Scientists now ask, "Did such animals actually exist in the Canyon at the time these drawings were made, or are these drawings merely the crude attempts of an inexperienced artist to portray a deer or a goat?"

A study of the travel records at Grand Canyon or of any other National Park will show at a glance how the automobile is becoming the popular means of travel to the Parks. Each year the percentage of auto tourists increases at an almost unbelievable rate, while the number of tourists coming by rail increases much less rapidly.

New demands of these sagebrushers must be met. Roadways must be improved, widened, paved, and kept free from snow. Nevertheless, the Service keeps continually in mind its well-established policy that a National Park should remain essentially as a wilderness area, that it should be left in so far as possible in its natural pristine state, a haunt for the nature lover, a sanctuary for wild life, and a resort where one may get away from the hurly-burly of civilization and the honk of an auto horn.

Hermit Rim Road, the first to be established, was built for horse-drawn vehicles. In fact, automobiles were not permitted on this road until many years later. With the establishment of the Park, it was turned over to the Federal Government. When this road was built, it was considered a marvel of engineering skill. That it was well built by competent engineers is indicated by the fact that it is still in constant use with but little improvement outside of ordinary maintenance.

However, it was built without thought of automobile traffic and it is, of course, considerably below the standards to which present-day auto roads are constructed. One of the items in the Park road program is the rebuilding of this particular road, cutting down its grades, widening and easing its many sharp curves.

Although the road construction program for Grand Canyon National Park as it now stands involves expenditures of several million dollars, there is but one short spur, some two miles, from Neal Springs to Point Imperial on the North Rim, which is an entirely new road.

All of the other items are for relocating, widening, paving, and improving roads to sections of the Park which, since the Park was established, have been accessible by primitive roads or wagon tracks, winding through the timber.

VI. WILD LIFE OF THE GRAND CANYON

"Does anything grow down there?"

Many a visitor, gazing over the South Rim at the miles upon miles of colored rock, has asked that question. The scene is one of desolation so far as plant and animal life are concerned, except for the few trees and shrubs near the rim.

As one examines the rocky barrenness of the earth's surface, it seems improbable that it could support vegetation of any kind. However, even when one is looking down into the Canyon from above, innumerable, somber, gray-green dots are seen to cover the landscape, and upon closer approach these dots take the form of low-lying, thorny shrubs, stunted by drouth, their leaf surfaces reduced to make for a minimum of evaporation.

To answer the oft-repeated question, yes, many things, both plant and animal, grow down there. Because of its peculiar formation, the Canyon holds a spell for the botanist almost equal to its lure for the geologist. Because of the great altitudinal range in the park, there is a variation in the temperature and a corresponding variation in both the plant and the animal life to be found. At the western boundary of the park the elevation of the Colorado River is only 1,780 feet above sea-level. Certain areas on the North Rim are well above 9,000 feet.

In making a trip across the Canyon and in ascending from the river to the North Rim, one passes through all the life zones that would be found in making a trip from central Mexico into central Canada.

Few localities show life zones more distinct and extreme than the Grand Canyon and there are few places on earth where in so short a distance there could be found the plants and animals characteristic of these widely varying climates. Each has its own distinctive and peculiar flora and fauna, and it is most interesting to the observing traveler to note the changes as different levels are reached.

Beginning at the bottom of the Canyon we have a broad area of the Lower Sonoran zone with a temperature and climate similar to that of central Mexico and with the plant and animal life common to that section of the country. In the Canyon this particular zone reaches from the river up to approximately the 4,000-foot contour on the north slope exposures and to the 5,000-foot level on the south slope exposures. In general this zone is from two to four miles wide, but extending back into side canyons it may reach a much greater width. It is characterized by a hot and dry climate, such as is found on the Colorado and Mojave deserts and in the Death Valley region.

The flora of the Lower Sonoran zone is of particular interest, not only to the nature student and botanist but also to the casual observer. Profuse and rank growth is not in evidence. The general similarity in the color of the flora deceives one as to its many varieties.

In one respect they are nearly all similar; they are almost universally equipped with thorns or "stickers" of some kind, the better to protect themselves from their enemies. Their existence is precarious enough, to say the least, and Nature seems to have made them as uninviting as possible both to man and to browsing animals, the better that they mav live, mature, and reproduce their kind.

Such plants as are not equipped with thorns are usually strongly aromatic and even bitter to the taste, unpalatable as forage crops. One old-timer says that all life at the bottom of the Canyon, whether plant or animal in nature, either "pricks, bites, or stings."

By far the most abundant plant in this region is the "Burro Brush," which is characteristic of practically the entire area and which covers the entire Tonto Plateau, not in thickets, but standing apart as individual plants, a characteristic of desert vegetation.

One of the few true acacias indigenous to the United States is found in this region, the *Acacia greggii* or "Cat's-Claw"—a very appropriate name indeed, since the many hooked spines on the twigs of this shrub, almost a small tree, are as sharp as the claws of a cat. This is a much-branched shrub attaining a height of ten to fifteen feet and a diameter of from four to six inches. Its flat, brown, nearly circular seeds are borne in pods. The wood is hard and durable, although its small size and inaccessibility render it of little or no value for commercial use. It is, however, much prized as fuel, burning with a bluish flame and making a fine bed of coals.

Like the cat's-claw, the mesquite also grows to a size almost classing it as a small tree. This is one of the most valuable of desert plants, since its seed and its seed pods are very palatable, rich in sugar content, and highly prized as food both by the Indians and by animals. Desert cattle and burros are particularly fond of the mesquite pods.

Among other shrubs of this region are Rabbit Brush, Wild Grape, Manzanita, and Mountain Mahogany, although the last two extend also into the next zone above.

Suspension Bridge, over which Kaibab Trail crosses the Colorado

Photo by Homer S. Jones

Bright Angel Canyon from Grand Canyon Lodge

Photo by Homer S. Jones

Changing colors as the shadows shift, Bright Angel Canyon (from same point)

In fact many of the plants and animals are not confined to one zone, but overlap the adjoining zone. This is true as well of the trees of the Lower Sonoran zone, some of which are found extending well into the Upper Sonoran zone.

Among them are Box Elder, Western Birch, two species of Willows, the Wilcox (Live) Oak, the Redbud or Judas tree, and, of course, the Cottonwood, which is found growing along the stream beds. The redbud in full bloom early in May is one of the most beautiful and striking sights to be seen in the entire Grand Canyon region.

During late April and early May, the lower stretches of the Canyon and the Tonto Plateau are a riot of color with wild flowers which bloom in profusion in the barren soil and dry climate and have the brilliant coloring characteristic of desert wild flowers.

Among the most common flowers to be found there are Wild Four-o'clock, Jimson Weed, Blue Larkspur, Scarlet Mallow, Milkweed, Wild Mustard, Nightshade, Indian Paint Brush, White Pentstemon, Prickly Phlox, Primrose, Wild Sweet Pea, and Poppy Thistle.

One interesting plant found in both of the Sonoran zones is Mormon Tea, sometimes known as Brigham Tea. It is one of the few remaining members of the ancient joint-fir family. Mormon Tea was so named because the plant was used in the preparation of a refreshing, non-intoxicating beverage during the early days when the Mormon people settled the surrounding country. It really makes a very pleasant and refreshing hot drink, a good substitute for tea. In the cook tent of any construction camp, there may be found always on the stove a pot of steeping "Mormon Tea" available for the men any time they come in from work.

Some of the most interesting types of plant life are the cacti and those desert species, such as the Narrow-leaved Yucca or the Mescal (*Agave utahensis*), which formed such an important article in the diet of both prehistoric and present-day Indians.

Several species of cacti are typical of this Lower Sonoran zone; among these are the so-called Barrel Cactus, the Hedgehog Cactus, the Banana Cactus, and two varieties of the Prickly Pear. In no hothouse or cultivated rose garden can be found blooms more delicate and beautiful than those on the various cacti. They first appear at the bottom of the Canyon in early April in a great variety of colors and shades—yellow, pink, red, purple, and mauve. A great patch of cactus in full bloom is one of the rarest and most beautiful sights that Mother Nature has to offer.

As might be expected, there are reptiles of many kinds to be found in the desert-like lower reaches of the Canyon. It might also be naturally expected that this region would be literally infested with rattlesnakes, but such is not the case. A species known as the Great Plains Rattlesnake inhabits that region and several specimens have been collected. These snakes, however, are quite rare and it is seldom that the ordinary tourist has an opportunity of seeing one. In fact, even the guides and rangers seldom see more than two or three rattlers in the course of an entire season.

The harmless and beautifully marked King Snake is frequently to be seen near the bottom of the Canyon. There are a great many lizards, mainly the Whip-tailed,

Large Scaly, and Western Collared varieties. These may be seen scurrying in every direction as one goes down the trail, and an occasional glimpse is had of the large fat Chuckwalla.

Among the mammals to be found in this region are the Antelope, the Free-tailed Bat, the Little Canyon Bat, the Pocket Gopher, the Cliff Mouse, the Desert Harvest Mouse, the Intermediate Pocket Mouse, and the Desert Wood Rat.

The Upper Sonoran zone covers both slopes of the Grand Canyon above the Lower Sonoran, or from about 4,000 to 6,000 feet on north slope exposures, and from 5,000 to 7,000 feet on south slope exposures, varying greatly with the steepness of the slopes. It is generally characterized by the nut pines and junipers.

There are two varieties of the so-called nut or piñon pines, one with two needles in a bundle, and the other the single-leaf type, both bearing an edible nut or seed.

In addition to the more common Utah Juniper, there is a species of this variety known to the botanist as *Juniperus scopularum,* the common name for which is the Rocky Mountain Red Cedar.

Other trees and shrubs characteristic of this zone are: two kinds of Ash, a prickly-leaved Live Oak, the Small-leaved Mountain Mahogany, the Cliff Rose, the Apache Plume, the Fringe Bush or Silk Tassel, the Snowberry, the Oregon Grape, the Fern Bush, and the Manzanita.

Several species of cacti are also common to this zone, such as Pincushion Cactus, Tree Cactus, and one of the Prickly Pears. Here, too, is found the *Yucca baccata* or Soapweed.

The Upper Sonoran zone is also rich in the growth of flowering annuals, among which are the Brownweed, Wild Buckwheat, Filaree, Blue Flax, Whip-lash Fleabane, Goldenrod, Wild Geranium, Sego Lily (the state flower of Utah), Golden Sage, Solomon's Seal, Bedstraw, and Sulphur Flower.

Reptiles of the zone include several species of the horned toad, a little sand lizard, a collared lizard, and the Bull Snake.

Mammals common to this zone in the park are Antelope, Bats (several species), Ring-tailed Cat, Gila Chipmunk, Small Gray Fox, Big-eared Mouse, Rowley White-footed Mouse, Flat-tailed Wood Rat, Round-tailed Wood Rat, Mountain Sheep, Spotted Skunk, and Rock Squirrel.

Above the Upper Sonoran zone, the Transition zone extends to an altitude of about 7,500 feet. This is characterized by the Yellow Pine, Gamble's Oak, Western Ironwood, several flowering locusts, Service Berry, and many other shrubs and flowering plants.

Flowers common to this region are Alpine Betony, Scarlet Bugler, Canyon Lupine, Blue Pentstemon, and Loco Weed.

Its mammals are the Large Brown Bat, the Fulvous Pocket Gopher, the Rufus Deer Mouse, the Porcupine, the Bushy-tailed Wood Rat, the Abert Squirrel, the Arizona Ground Squirrel, and the Kaibab Squirrel.

On the Kaibab plateau the Canadian zone covers the high country from about 7,500 feet on northeast slopes and from 8,500 feet on southwest slopes, up to the highest parts, at about 9,000 feet. On the steep Canyon walls facing the northwest, strips of Canadian species extend along the base of sheer cliffs much lower down, and in many cases to below the Transition zone species, which cover the more rounded slopes above. In some places these Canadian zone strips reach even to the level of the Upper Sonoran zone on opposite slopes facing the warm rays of the sun.

Many of these Canadian zone strips show under the rim of the Canyon along both sides, and may tend to confuse the observer unless their origin is understood. Generally, they are where the rays of the sun never shine, or where it touches for only a short time during some part of the day. Often they are where snow drifts over in winter and lies until late in spring, keeping the ground cool and moist.

Trees common to this zone are the Douglas Fir, the Engelmann Spruce, the Colorado Blue Spruce, and the Quaking Aspen.

The zone has no reptiles, and its mammals are the Lynx Cat, the Colorado Chipmunk, the Mule Deer, the Colorado Pocket Gopher, the Mountain Lion, and the Spruce Squirrel.

On the North Rim, especially during the rainy season, there is found an abundance of mushrooms. These are considered a great delicacy by the deer.

It is worth while to note that at least one tree of this zone, the Douglas Fir, and, very rarely, the Colorado Blue Spruce, is found on the South Rim. This is accounted for by the fact that on shaded slopes below the rim with a northern exposure, there are found conditions similar to those of a higher zone. These trees may sometimes be found within two or three feet of the rim, but they are never found on top of the South Rim.

One of the most interesting trees in Grand Canyon National Park is the Ironwood, or Knowlton's Hornbeam (*Ostrya knowltoni*). The type specimen was first collected by Mr. F. H. Knowlton, for whom it was named, near the end of the Hance Trail, in September 1889. After this species was first described, several botanists came to Grand Canyon to find more specimens but failed to locate any trace of the tree. It was therefore feared by some to have become extinct. In recent years, however, it has been found at several places in the Grand Canyon, in Oak Creek Canyon, and in southern Utah. With the opening of the new Kaibab Trail to the North Rim, several hundred of these trees were found near Roaring Springs, hitherto practically inaccessible; needless to say, this "find" delighted botanists and lovers of trees.

Grand Canyon National Park is rich in its bird life, nearly one hundred and forty species having been found and identified there. Among the more common of these are the following:

Western Bluebird
Mountain Chicadee
Mourning Dove
House Finch
Yellow-shafted Flicker
Pale Goldfinch
Black-headed Grosbeak
Red-tailed Hawk
Sparrow Hawk
Broad-tailed Hummingbird
Long-crested Jay
Piñon Jay
Red-backed Junco
Pigmy Nuthatch
Slender-billed Nuthatch
Water Ouzel
Western Robin
Western Chipping Sparrow
Violet-green Swallow
White-throated Swift
Western Tanager
Gray Titmouse
Spurred Towhee
Audubon Warbler
Black-throated Gray Warbler
Gairdner Woodpecker
Canyon Wren
Rock Wren

Among other birds to be found in the park are the Golden Eagle, Dusky Grouse, Gambel's Quail, and Road-Runner. These are by no means as common as those above listed but they are all most interesting.

To the traveler approaching the North Rim of the Grand Canyon from Zion and Bryce Canyon National Parks, and from southern Utah, the limitless Kaibab Forest is a welcome transition from the tropic climate of the desert and the Prismatic Plains, crossed in the vicinity of Kanab and Fredonia, or Pipe Spring National Monument. The high, dry, bracing, pine-laden air, the dim forest aisles, and the frequent glimpses of wild deer and white-tailed squirrels make the road to the North Rim a fitting prelude to the silent symphony of the Grand Canyon itself.

Kaibab is a Piute Indian word meaning "mountain-lying-down," a description that fits it well. It is a vast plateau, some 50 miles long and 35 miles wide, containing approximately 500 square miles of Yellow Pine, White and Douglas Fir, Engelmann and Colorado Blue Spruce—the largest and most beautiful virgin forest in the United States.

The picturesque charm of this dense forest of dark evergreens is greatly enhanced by an understory of quaking aspen, with its white, birch-like bark and light green leaves attached to the twigs in such a manner that even the slightest breeze sets them all to "quaking," or trembling. This picture is even more beautiful in the early fall after the first frosts have touched the quaking aspens, turning these leaves to every shade, from a bright golden yellow to a deep burnt orange.

A strip of the Kaibab Forest extending northward from the rim of the Canyon for a distance of from ten to twelve miles is within Grand Canyon National Park. The remainder of this forest, northward as far as the desert slopes, is in the Kaibab National Forest, and is administered by the Forest Service, a bureau of the Department of Agriculture.

There is no national park, and indeed no section of the United States, where deer are to be seen in such large numbers and over so great an area, as in the Kaibab Forest. It has been estimated that approximately 30,000 Kaibab mule deer (*Odocoileus hemionus macrotis*) roam this range. They are large and unafraid, not to the extent that they can be approached and petted as tame deer, but they have become so accustomed to the presence of human beings that one may approach to within twenty or thirty yards of them before they take to their heels and scamper off through the woods.

During the day they are to be found singly or in small groups throughout the dense forest, where they have sought shelter from the sun. In the evening, however, they congregate in large numbers in the open park-like meadows to feed on a short, sweet mountain clover, of which they are particularly fond. At such times one may count many bands of from fifty to two hundred in the meadows through which the approach road runs.

So accustomed are these deer to passing automobiles that they are undisturbed and graze contentedly within a few yards of the road, never even lifting their heads as the automobiles whiz by. A late evening drive from Grand Canyon Lodge on the North Rim northward, say to VT Ranch, enables one to see many hundreds of these deer along the road, and frequently visitors have reported counting more than a thousand deer in this eighteen-mile drive.

The deer continue their grazing on their especial delicacy, the mountain clover, until well toward morning. Headlights flashed on a band of grazing deer, as one rounds a turn in the road, will reveal dozens of pair of eyes reflecting like tiny ruby lamps in the darkness.

As winter approaches, the Kaibab herd migrates from the top of the mountain to the winter range on the desert slopes, far outside the National Park. All hunting is, of course, prohibited within the park, but after the deer leave their summer range and begin to drift out of the park toward the deserts, serious inroads on the herd are made by the hunters.

Early in June the mother does appear with their fawns. These babies are prominently marked with spots, which remain until the animals are several months old, and it is a noteworthy fact that a spotted fawn has no scent. This seems to be a wise provision of Nature to protect the deer from their predatory enemies during infancy.

A fawn, when even a few hours old, can literally "run like a deer." During the early summer there are always a number of experienced trappers engaged in catching young fawns. This work, which is carried on outside the National Park, is done with the aid of dogs trained to catch the young deer and hold them down on the ground under their fore paws until the trapper can arrive. The dogs seem to understand thoroughly that the fawns are not to be harmed.

The fawns are then taken to prepared pens at a central point and raised on cow's milk until late fall, when they are shipped to both public and private zoos and game refuges throughout the country. The fawns are easily tamed, and make excellent pets. Within a few hours after they are captured and turned loose in the pens they become accustomed to the touch of human hands and will follow their captors around like dogs.

Although deer on the South Rim are comparatively rare, a number of Kaibab fawns are loosed there each year. A band of these now quite tame young deer may be seen at almost any time by visitors to Grand Canyon Village.

An interesting sidelight on the ways of the deer was offered during the late fall of 1924, when the famous Kaibab deer drive was organized. It was proposed to round up a great number of these deer on their native range in the same manner as range cattle, drive them down Nankoweap Creek, swim them across the river, and take them on up to the South Rim.

Hundreds of Indians and cowboys were engaged for this gigantic round-up, much publicity was given to the affair, and the net result was that there were almost as many motion picture cameras in evidence as there were deer. In spite of the fact that the promoters had made enthusiastic promises to deliver 10,000 wild deer to the South Rim at one dollar per head, not a single deer even saw the trail leading into the Canyon from the North Rim.

There were many alibis for the failure of the drive, among them "lack of proper organization" and the fact that a great storm broke at a critical moment. These were probably contributory, but the fundamental reason was simply that deer are easy enough to drive only so long as they are being "driven" in the particular direction that they want to be going. However, there could never be gathered together a band of mounted Indians and cowboys of sufficient size to make them leave their home range.

The Kaibab herd has increased rapidly with the reduction in the number of cougars, or mountain lions, on the North Rim by lion hunters. One of the most famous of the North Rim lion hunters was "Uncle Jimmy" Owens, who was President Roosevelt's guide during his Kaibab hunting trip. Uncle Jimmy has accounted for around 1,200 lions, and his famous lion dog, "Pot," has played his rôle at the death of more than five hundred of these cruel animals.

Next to the deer, the most interesting species of wild life on the North Rim is the Kaibab White-tailed Squirrel (*Sciurus kaibabensis*). This is undoubtedly the most beautiful squirrel in the Western Hemisphere, and its range is limited exclusively to this particular forested area.

The White-tailed Squirrel is about the same size as its near relative, the Abert Squirrel, found on the South Rim. Its body is a dark bluish-gray, marked with brown, and its most striking characteristic is a long, broad, feathery tail that is almost pure white.

The Kaibab and the Abert are the only American squirrels with conspicuous ear tufts and they have many other similar characteristics. Their nesting habits are much the same; they both have a similar call or bark; and they both assume the attitude of the flying squirrel when leaping from branch to branch.

Originally they were undoubtedly the same species, the radical change in the markings having been brought about by the factor of isolation due to the cutting of the Canyon. In their present habitat they are completely isolated from the rest of the world by the Grand Canyon on one side and by deserts on the other three sides. This tends to curtail any migration and accounts for the fact that this species is found nowhere else in the world.

Another instance in which the canyon walls act as a barrier to migration is in the case of the raccoon found in Havasu Canyon. There this animal is found in comparatively large numbers, and, although there are many other side canyons in which there exist conditions favorable to the raccoon, this is the only side canyon within the park where this particular form of animal life is found.

Still another species of animal life which has had a considerable influence on the natural features of the park is the common burro. Although these animals were not native to the Canyon, large numbers of them were abandoned in the early days at the foot of the old trails by prospectors. Left there to make their own living, they increased rapidly until hundreds of them ranged over the Tonto Plateau and in the many side canyons. Since there was no new stock introduced, these animals became inbred and stunted.

The scanty vegetation of the region afforded but little forage, and as the numbers increased many of them literally starved to death. When flowers, weeds, and small shrubs had been exhausted, they turned to the brush and trees, with the final result that this portion of their range became almost denuded of every form of vegetation.

They became a serious nuisance to the pack trains operating in the Canyon and even a menace to the safety of riders making the trail trips. As the saddle and pack mules would come unexpectedly on a band of wild burros or as they would be startled by a sudden volley of brays from an opposite side hill, they would frequently shy so suddenly as to unseat their riders.

Finally, the rangers undertook to rid the Canyon of this undesirable species of animal life, with the thought that, relieved from this intensive grazing, the range would restock itself and perhaps furnish sufficient forage to attract deer, mountain sheep, or antelope.

The rangers organized themselves into burro-hunting parties and practically exterminated the pests. As a result, the Plateau has very largely been restocked by Nature with flowers and various forms of vegetation common to that region, so that it is once more a riot of color during the spring season.

The National Park Service has undertaken an extensive educational program, not only in Grand Canyon, but also in other National Parks. Naturalists conduct research work, collect specimens, arrange exhibits, and assist visitors to enjoy the geologic, historical, and wild life stories of the Parks. At Grand Canyon, one trained naturalist is assigned exclusively to this line of work throughout the entire year. During the summer he is assisted by temporary ranger-naturalists, one of whom is assigned to such work exclusively on the North Rim.

Ranger-naturalist headquarters on the South Rim are at the Yavapai Point trail-side museum, or observation station, one and one-half miles east of El Tovar, provided through the co-operation of the Laura Spelman Rockefeller Foundation, the National Academy of Sciences, the Carnegie Institution, and other organizations interested in the advancement of science. In it are located models, charts, maps, and specimens revealing the fascinating story of Grand Canyon.

Informal lectures are given frequently during the day at

the Yavapai Station by the Park naturalist. During the summer season many of the most famous scientists of the country visit the Canyon for the purpose of pursuing their studies and to assist in carrying out this great educational program. Frequently the visitor has the opportunity of hearing talks at the Yavapai Station by these noted men of science.

Each summer evening around a huge camp-fire at the public camp ground a Park naturalist or a visiting scientist talks. On the North Rim, these nature lectures are given each evening in the recreation room of Grand Canyon Lodge. There are also nature-guide walks conducted from each rim. The ranger-naturalists conduct parties of visitors along the trails on the rims of the Canyon, pointing out on the ground the various geologic formations, the different forms of plant and animal life, and other features of interest.

The Grand Canyon is one of Mother Nature's most absorbing "story books." There's many a tale to be unfolded by the rocks, the streams, the trees, the flowers, or the alert creatures that live in the fairyland of the tinted cliffs and the rose-hued castles. The leaves of the Grand Canyon story book are always open to one with enough curiosity to turn the pages.

VII. SOMETHING NEW EVERY DAY

"How long does it take to see the Grand Canyon?"

That is one of our most popular questions, and a hard one to answer. There have been speedy "sagebrushers" who have dashed up to the South Rim, looked over, and then sped away to say that they have seen the Grand Canyon. They caught a glimpse of it—that is all.

Many a traveler arrives on the morning train and leaves in the evening. To see the Canyon that way is better than not seeing it at all, but not much better.

That memorable first glimpse of the Grand Canyon is something burned into the memory for a lifetime. There is nothing on this round planet quite so staggering in its immensity, so marvelous in its maze of colors, so awe-inspiring in its silence.

Yet, in spite of that first impression of pastel immobility, the Canyon is alive and ever-changing, as has been discovered by all who have thoroughly "seen" it in its changing moods and hues. In the Canyon and the fascinating country surrounding it, there is something different to be discovered every new day.

Many are they who have acquired the Grand Canyon habit, returning each year to follow old trails, either afoot, or on mule back. Some arrange independent pack trips lasting any length of time from a few days to several weeks.

The South Rim may be visited any day of the year. Trains arrive at El Tovar daily. Motor roads are kept open the year around.

The North Rim resort season is from June 1 to October 1. Being higher in elevation, snows make motor travel difficult in winter. North Rim may be reached by trail during the winter, but accommodations are not available.

"What are the accommodations?"

At the South Rim is the El Tovar, an American-plan hotel, situated at the top of the Canyon wall. It is operated by the Fred Harvey Company, which likewise operates Bright Angel Cottages, a camp with both tents and bungalows, on the European plan, and the Housekeeping Camp, where visitors may stop with a minimum of expense. For those wishing to camp out, there is the Government camp ground, where no charge is made and where the motorist may pitch his own tent. At South Rim is a grocery store, a garage, a studio, a souvenir shop, and a delicatessen shop.

In the Canyon itself are Phantom Ranch and Hermit Camp, American-plan lodges, maintained by Fred Harvey and offering excellent accommodations and good meals.

At the North Rim is the magnificent Grand Canyon Lodge, built by the Union Pacific, and operated on the American plan by the Utah Parks Company, a subsidiary corporation. Here also are a public camp ground, a store, a studio, a cafeteria, and a garage.

Motor transportation is provided on the South Rim by the Fred Harvey Company and on the North Rim by the Utah Parks Company. Both companies maintain saddle animals for pack trips on the rim in their respective areas. Trips into the Canyon from either rim are conducted by Fred Harvey.

All rates and prices are established by the National Park Service of the Department of the Interior.

Fred Harvey Photo

Ribbon Falls in Havasu Canyon

Fred Harvey Photo

Interior of Hopi House, El Tovar

Hopi pueblo of Moenkopi, near the Painted Desert

Visitors wishing to do so may see the Canyon from an airplane operated by the Scenic Airways, from airports just outside the park. However, the planes are flown entirely on the responsibility of the Scenic Airways, Inc., without being subject to regulations of the National Park Service.

A Day at South Rim

Visitors may make the trip westward from El Tovar by motor or afoot to Hermit Rest, delightful rest and refreshment station of the Fred Harvey system, built in the cliff, with all the atmosphere of a cave but with great windows on one side enabling one to gaze across the Canyon. En route, see Powell Monument, and stop at several points for choice views of the Canyon.

Return to El Tovar in time for the 11:30 lecture at the Kolb Brothers studio, where may be seen motion pictures of the hazardous trip of the Brothers through the Grand Canyon in small boats.

Luncheon at El Tovar; then a drive through the forest to the east, stopping at Yavapai Point Observation Station, where the Park Naturalist will tell of the origin and the natural features of the Canyon. For spectacular Canyon views, stop also at Yaki Point, Grand View, Lipan Point, and Navajo Point, also known as Desert View, because of the remarkable long-range vista of the Painted Desert.

Return to El Tovar in time for the Hopi Indian dances at the Hopi House, opposite the hotel, at 5:30. At the Hopi House, a faithful reproduction of a Hopi pueblo, may be seen Indian baskets, blankets, and silver work. Just outside the Hopi House are several hogans erected by Navajos who ply their trades here.

After dinner, there is an illustrated lecture descriptive of the Canyon trips, in the music room of the hotel. During the summer months the park naturalist lectures at the public camp ground to visitors gathered about the great fire.

Bright Angel Trail Ride

For those who have but one day to make the trip, trail-riding parties with competent guides leave South Rim daily about nine in the morning, returning about five in the afternoon. This is a strenuous one-day trip, and visitors who can do so are urged to devote two days to the trip by mule back into the Canyon, stopping over night at Hermit Camp or Phantom Ranch. This trip is made likewise on foot by experienced hikers, who should remember, however, that in Grand Canyon, the usual order of mountain-climbing is reversed and the hard part is the up grade out of the Canyon. Hikers should conserve their strength for this "last long mile." Only those in good physical condition and accustomed to hiking at high altitudes should attempt the Canyon trails afoot.

Kaibab Trail Trip

From South Rim, the fascinating trip down the Kaibab Trail starts right after lunch, so that the trail rider may reach the lower walls of the Canyon when the shadows are longest and the colors are highest. Night is spent at the delightful Phantom Ranch, maintained by the Fred Harvey System, after crossing the river via the Kaibab Suspension Bridge. On the following day the return trip may be made in a leisurely manner, via the same route or across the Tonto Trail to Bright Angel Trail and thence to the South

Rim. This trip offers an exceptional opportunity to see the Canyon.

For those who can spend an extra day and night in the Canyon, the side trip from Phantom Ranch to Ribbon Falls and Roaring Springs is well worth while.

Hermit Trail Trip

The Hermit Trail trip, via mule, starts during the morning from South Rim, and the trail-rider remains over night in the Canyon at Hermit Camp. Return may be made the following day either via the same route or across the Tonto and up Bright Angel Trail. For those who can afford the time, the trip from Hermit Camp to Phantom Ranch is recommended on the second day, with an over-night stay at the latter camp the second night, and return to South Rim via the Kaibab Trail the third day.

Navahopi–Painted Desert Trip

The motor trip from South Rim, over the Navahopi Road, across the Painted Desert to the Tuba City Indian Reservation, and to Moenkopi, quaint Hopi pueblo, is one of the rarest experiences of a visit to the Grand Canyon Country. Starting at El Tovar, the road winds over mountains, through forests, across deserts, past Navajo flocks and hogans and isolated trading-posts, to the Little Colorado, which is crossed at Cameron Bridge; thence past petrified forests, tracks of ancient dinosaurs, and through weirdly colorful rock formations of the Painted Desert. At Moenkopi are seen the Hopis at their work, just as generations have labored before them, while Tuba City represents the modern Indian school.

This great trip may be made in one day, but at least two days should be devoted to it, if possible, the better to witness the magic of the Painted Desert and its people. Motorists may stay over night at trading-posts, an adventure in itself, and may, if they wish, cross the Canyon at the new Lee's Ferry Bridge and turn westward to North Rim. From Rim to Rim via this route is 236 miles.

Havasu Canyon Trip

For the visitor seeking adventure out of the ordinary, the Havasu Canyon trip, requiring at least three and preferably five days, is a rare one indeed. Here one visits perhaps the most primitive and isolated Indian settlement in the country, the Havasupai Reservation, located appropriately in a tiny fertile valley surrounded by Canyon walls. Through the valley flows Havasu Creek, which plunges over the cliffs in a series of three beautiful waterfalls.

This trip begins with a thirty-five mile motor trip from El Tovar to Hilltop, after which comes a fourteen-mile ride on Indian ponies down the old Indian trail, little touched by the hand of man. In the Canyon, visitors must camp out, there being no accommodations other than those which may be arranged extemporaneously. Arrangements for this trip must be made sufficiently far in advance to secure ponies from the Indian village and have them brought up to Hilltop.

A Day at North Rim

North Rim is reached by the visitor via motor stages of the Utah Parks Company from railhead at Cedar City, nearly two hundred miles away, or via private automobile from the Arrowhead Highway between Salt Lake City and southern California. The visit to North Rim is the "high spot" in the Union Pacific Utah Parks tour, including motor stage trip to Zion National Park, Pipe Spring National Monument, Bryce Canyon National Park, and Cedar Breaks.

The view from Grand Canyon Lodge, on the North Rim, at the head of Bright Angel Canyon, is one which holds the visitor spellbound for hours. The Lodge itself rises from the wall of the Canyon almost as if the harmonious structure were a natural part of the Canyon.

Foot and bridle trails extend from the Lodge along the rim and back through the pines and aspens of Kaibab Forest. North Rim being 1,300 feet higher than South Rim, its vegetation is much more dense. A ranger-naturalist is on hand at the North Rim to acquaint visitors with the lore of the Canyon and the forest.

North Rim Trail Trips

North Rim and the great Kaibab Forest make an ideal saddle-horse country, and no visit to that section of the Park is complete without a horseback trip through the great open forests of that region. Short trips from Grand Canyon Lodge may be made over bridle paths to Natchi and McKinnon Points, to Farview and to Point Imperial. Camping in the Kaibab is a delight to the lover of the open trail, and pack trips of almost any length, from two or three days up to a month or more, may be arranged to Cape Royal, Point Sublime, Powell Plateau, Thunder River, Nankoweap Creek, the Sand Rocks of wild horse fame, the Toroweap Valley, and scores of interesting out-of-the-way spots, among them some of the best-preserved ruins of prehistoric cliff dwellings in the park.

Saddle mules and guides are available for trips into the Canyon by way of the Kaibab Trail. A one-day trip may be made to Roaring Springs, or in two days the trip to the river by way of Ribbon Falls may be taken with a stop over night at Phantom Ranch, returning the following day either to the North Rim or continuing on over the Kaibab Suspension Bridge to the South Rim.

North Rim, with its winding trails through the sheltering, murmuring forests, all leading to ancient cliff dwellings, or high points jutting over the Canyon, and offering frequent spectacular vistas, is a paradise for the hiker as well as the trail rider. Thousands make the North Rim community, with its comfortable accommodations, the center from which to "hit the trail."

North Rim Motor Trips

Although development of roads and trails on the North Rim is comparatively recent, there are many trips that may be made by auto or by motor stages, notably those to Point Imperial, the highest point on either side of the Canyon, Farview, Cape Royal, and Point Sublime. From this side of the Canyon, too, Zion or Bryce Canyon National Park may be reached by private car or by the regular auto stages of the Union Pacific Company in a one-day trip over good roads. Automobile communication with the South Rim is had by way of Jacobs Lake, House Rock Valley, Lee's Ferry Bridge, and the Painted Desert country.

INDEX

Tillotson, Miner Raymond, 1886-
Grand canyon country, by M.R. Tillotson and Frank J. Taylor; foreword by Horace M. Albright. Stanford University, Calif., Stanford University Press, 1929.
108p. front., plates. 23cm.

Illustrated lining-papers.

1.Grand canyon. I.Taylor, Frank J., 1894- joint author. II.Title.

To Zion National Park
Kaibab
Nationa
Cliff Dwellings
Shinumo Amphitheater
Kaibab
Holy Grail Temple
Gatagama Pt.
Pahuta Pt.
Havasupai Indian Reservation
Great Thumb Pt.
Fossil Bay
Granite Gorge
Powell Plateau
Shinumo Creek
Pt. Sublime
Bright Angel Pt.
Shiva Temple
Buddha Temple
Hermit Falls
Isis Temple
Bright Angel Creek
Montezuma Pt.
Aztec Amphitheater
Apache Pt.
Hermit Cabins
Phantom Ranch
Suspension Bridge
Hopi Pt.
Hermit's Rest
El Tovar
Yavapai Pt.
Hopi House
Coconino
Plateau
N
W
E
S
Red Butte
Tusayan
Nationa